asian flavours

Published in 2008 by Murdoch Books Pty Limited.
www.murdochbooks.com.au

Murdoch Books Australia
Pier 8/9, 23 Hickson Road
Millers Point NSW 2000
Phone: + 61 (0) 2 8220 2000
Fax: + 61 (0) 2 8220 2558

Murdoch Books UK Limited
Erico House, 6th Floor
93–99 Upper Richmond Road
Putney, London SW15 2TG
Phone: + 44 (0) 20 8785 5995
Fax: + 44 (0) 20 8785 5985

Chief Executive: Juliet Rogers
Publishing Director: Kay Scarlett

Concept & Art Direction: Sarah Odgers
Design: Jacqueline Duncan
Project Manager: Rhiain Hull
Editor: Jacqueline Blanchard
Photographer: Jared Fowler
Stylist: Cherise Koch
Production: Monique Layt
Food preparation: Alan Wilson
Introduction text: Leanne Kitchen
Recipes developed by the Murdoch Books Test Kitchen

National Library of Australia Cataloguing-in-Publication Data

Asian flavours. Includes index.
ISBN 9781921259104 (pbk.).
1. Cookery, Asian. I. Price, Jane. (Series: Kitchen Classics; 8). 641.595
A catalogue record is available from the British Library.

Colour reproduction by Splitting Image Colour Studio, Melbourne, Australia.
Printed by 1010 Printing International Limited in 2008. PRINTED IN CHINA.
Reprinted 2008.

IMPORTANT: Those who might be at risk from the effects of salmonella poisoning (the elderly, pregnant woman, young children and those suffering from immune deficiency diseases) should consult their doctor with any concerns about eating raw eggs.

CONVERSION GUIDE: You may find cooking times vary depending on the oven you are using. For fan-forced ovens, as a general rule, set the oven temperature to 20°C (35°F) lower than indicated in the recipe. We have used 20 ml (4 teaspoon) tablespoon measures. If you are using a 15 ml (3 teaspoon) tablespoon, for most recipes the difference will not be noticeable. However, for recipes using baking powder, gelatine, bicarbonate of soda (baking soda), small amounts of flour, add an extra teaspoon for each tablespoon specified.

asian flavours

THE ASIAN RECIPES YOU MUST HAVE

SERIES EDITOR **JANE PRICE**

MURDOCH BOOKS

CONTENTS

HOT WOKS AND CHOPSTICKS

It's true the world is shrinking. Affordable air travel and information superhighways can either take us to the world or, in the case of TV and the internet, bring the world to us. The result of this for the cook is unparalleled access to international cuisines and for many kitchen mavens, learning about myriad types of Asian foods has been an inspiring journey into little-known territory. Western versions of Chinese dishes and Indian curries have long been known, but delving deeper into the Asian region to discover 'real' Thai, Vietnamese, Korean, Japanese, Indonesian and Malaysian food is like unlocking Pandora's box. Inside is a world of fragrance, flavour, texture and colour that is quite unlike any other; cooking in the Asian manner fills a kitchen with exotic smells, sounds and sensations. There is something alluring about the perfumed aromas that rise when lemon grass, ginger, coriander or lime are chopped and sliced. Slurping up soft, velvety rice noodles, snacking on freshly-made spring rolls or sweating over a complex, spicy curry are always stimulating dining experiences.

One of the best things about cooking Asian is that much of the hard work (chopping, grinding, slicing, pounding, wrapping) can be done in advance; a few flourishes, a little last-minute frying or steaming, a final stir of the curry or braise, some speedy arranging in bowls or on platters and *voilà*. A feast from the East is ready! Whether it's a filling mid-week meal of chilli beef, rogan josh or chicken chow mein, or a sumptuous, themed Thai, Indian or Vietnamese buffet for a special occasion, there has never been a better reason to break out the chopsticks and fire up the wok than the recipes awaiting you in *Kitchen Classics' Asian Flavours*!

CRISPY CRUNCHY

CHINESE SPRING ROLLS

2 dried shiitake mushrooms
250 g (9 oz) minced (ground) pork
1½ tablespoons dark soy sauce
2 teaspoons dry sherry
½ teaspoon Chinese five-spice
2 tablespoons cornflour (cornstarch), plus 1½ teaspoons, extra
80 ml (2½ fl oz/⅓ cup) peanut oil
½ celery stalk, finely chopped
2 spring onions (scallions), thinly sliced
30 g (1 oz) tinned bamboo shoots, finely sliced
40 g (1½ oz/¾ cup) shredded Chinese cabbage (wong bok)
2 garlic cloves, crushed
2 teaspoons finely chopped fresh ginger
¼ teaspoon sugar
¼ teaspoon sesame oil
250 g (9 oz) packet 12 cm (4½ inch) square spring roll wrappers
oil, for deep-frying

DIPPING SAUCE
2 tablespoons soy sauce
1 tablespoon hoisin sauce
1 tablespoon plum sauce
1 tablespoon sweet chilli sauce

MAKES 30

Put the shiitake mushrooms in a heatproof bowl, cover with boiling water and soak for 20 minutes. Squeeze the mushrooms dry, discard the stems and thinly slice the caps.

Mix the pork, soy sauce, sherry, five-spice and 1 tablespoon of the cornflour in a non-metallic bowl. Leave for 15 minutes.

Heat 2 tablespoons of the peanut oil in a wok over high heat until nearly smoking, then add the celery, spring onion, bamboo shoots and Chinese cabbage and stir-fry for 3–4 minutes, or until just soft. Season with salt, then transfer to a bowl and set aside.

Heat the remaining peanut oil in the wok and cook the garlic and ginger for 30 seconds. Add the pork mixture and stir-fry for 2–3 minutes, or until nearly cooked. Combine 1½ teaspoons of the cornflour with 60 ml (2 fl oz/¼ cup) water. Return the cooked vegetables to the wok, then stir in the mushrooms. Add the sugar, sesame oil and cornflour mixture and stir for 2 minutes. Remove from the heat and cool.

To make the dipping sauce, combine the soy sauce, hoisin sauce, plum sauce, sweet chilli sauce and 80 ml (2½ fl oz/⅓ cup) water in a bowl and stir to combine.

Make a paste with the remaining cornflour and 2–3 teaspoons cold water. Place a spring roll wrapper on a work surface, with one corner pointing towards you. Put 2 teaspoons of the filling in the centre of the wrapper, then brush the edges with a little cornflour paste. Roll up, tucking in the sides as you do so. Repeat with the remaining filling and wrappers.

Fill a wok or deep heavy-based saucepan one-third full of oil and heat to 180°C (350°F), or until a cube of bread dropped into the oil browns in 15 seconds. Deep-fry the spring rolls in batches until golden, then drain on crumpled paper towel. Serve hot with the dipping sauce.

PREPARATION TIME: 45 MINUTES +   COOKING TIME: 20 MINUTES

SALT AND PEPPER SQUID

1 kg (2 lb 4 oz) squid tubes, halved lengthways
250 ml (9 fl oz/1 cup) lemon juice
250 g (9 oz/2 cups) cornflour (cornstarch)
1 tablespoon ground white pepper
2 teaspoons caster (superfine) sugar
4 egg whites, lightly beaten
oil, for deep-frying
lemon wedges, to serve
coriander (cilantro) leaves, to garnish

SERVES 10

Open out the squid tubes, wash them and pat dry. Lay on a chopping board with the inside facing upwards. Score a fine diamond pattern on the squid, being careful not to cut all the way through. Cut into 5 x 3 cm (2 x 1¼ inch) pieces. Place in a flat non-metallic dish and pour the lemon juice over. Cover and refrigerate for 15 minutes. Drain and pat dry.

Combine the cornflour, 1 tablespoon salt, white pepper and sugar in a bowl. Dip the squid into the egg white and dust with the flour mixture.

Fill a wok or deep heavy-based saucepan one-third full of oil and heat to 180°C (350°F), or until a cube of bread dropped into the oil browns in 15 seconds. Deep-fry the squid in batches for 1–2 minutes, or until the squid turns white and curls. Drain on crumpled paper towel and serve immediately.

PREPARATION TIME: 30 MINUTES +   COOKING TIME: 10 MINUTES

TEMPURA PRAWNS

12 large raw prawns (shrimp)
oil, for deep-frying
1 egg
250 ml (9 fl oz/1 cup) iced water
125 g (4½ oz/1 cup) tempura flour, sifted
2 ice cubes
1 sheet toasted nori, shredded

SERVES 4

Peel the prawns and gently pull out the dark vein from each prawn back, starting from the head end, leaving the tails intact. Using a sharp knife, make three or four diagonal cuts in the underside of each prawn one-third of the way through. Pat the prawns dry with paper towel.

Fill a wok or deep heavy-based saucepan one-third full of oil and heat to 180°C (350°F), or until a cube of bread dropped into the oil browns in 15 seconds.

While the oil is heating, put the egg in a large bowl and, using chopsticks or a fork, break it up. Add the iced water and mix well with chopsticks. Add the sifted flour all at once and mix with chopsticks until just combined, then add the ice cubes — the mixture should be lumpy.

Dip the prawns in the batter and deep-fry in batches, four at a time, drizzling with some of the remaining batter to give a spiky effect. Cook for 1 minute, or until crisp. Drain the prawns on crumpled paper towel, sprinkle with the nori and serve immediately.

PREPARATION TIME: 25 MINUTES   COOKING TIME: 10 MINUTES

SAMOSAS

CUCUMBER RAITA

2 Lebanese (short) cucumbers, peeled, seeded and finely chopped
250 g (9 oz/1 cup) plain yoghurt
1 teaspoon ground cumin
1 teaspoon mustard seeds
½ teaspoon grated fresh ginger

1 tablespoon vegetable oil
1 onion, chopped
1 teaspoon grated fresh ginger
1 garlic clove, crushed
2 teaspoons ground coriander
2 teaspoons ground cumin
2 teaspoons garam masala
1½ teaspoons chilli powder
¼ teaspoon ground turmeric
300 g (10½ oz) potatoes, cut into 1 cm (½ inch) cubes and boiled
40 g (1½ oz/⅓ cup) frozen peas
2 tablespoons chopped coriander (cilantro) leaves
1 teaspoon lemon juice
6 sheets ready-rolled puff pastry
oil, for deep-frying

MAKES 24

To make the raita, put the cucumber and yoghurt in a bowl and mix together well.

Dry-fry the cumin and mustard seeds in a small frying pan over medium heat for 1 minute, or until fragrant and lightly browned, then add to the yoghurt mixture. Stir in the ginger, season to taste with salt and freshly ground black pepper, and mix together well. Refrigerate until needed.

Heat a wok over medium heat, add the oil and swirl to coat the base and side. Add the onion, ginger and garlic and cook for 2 minutes, or until softened. Add the spices, boiled potato, peas and 2 teaspoons water. Cook for 1 minute, or until all the moisture evaporates. Remove from the heat and stir in the coriander leaves and lemon juice.

Cut out 12 rounds from the pastry sheets using a 12.5 cm (5 inch) cutter, then cut each round in half. Shape 1 semi-circle into a cone, wet the edges and seal the side seam, leaving an opening large enough for the filling. Spoon 3 teaspoons of the filling into the cone, then seal. Repeat to make 23 more samosas.

Fill a wok or deep heavy-based saucepan one-third full of oil and heat to 180°C (350°F), or until a cube of bread dropped into the oil browns in 15 seconds. Cook the samosas in batches for 1–2 minutes, or until golden. Drain on crumpled paper towel and season. Serve with the chilled cucumber raita.

PREPARATION TIME: 30 MINUTES   COOKING TIME: 25 MINUTES

NOTE: Raita can be made ahead of time and stored in the refrigerator in an airtight container for up to 3 days.

STUFFED CHICKEN WINGS

12 large chicken wings
20 g (3/4 oz) dried rice vermicelli
1 tablespoon grated palm sugar (jaggery)
2 tablespoons fish sauce
200 g (7 oz) minced (ground) pork
2 spring onions (scallions), chopped
3 garlic cloves, chopped
1 small red chilli, chopped
3 tablespoons chopped coriander
(cilantro) leaves
peanut oil, for deep-frying
rice flour, well seasoned, to coat
chilli sauce or sweet chilli sauce, to serve

MAKES 12

Using a small sharp knife and starting at the fatter end of the wing, scrape down the bone, pushing the flesh and skin as you go until you reach the connecting joint. Twist and pull the exposed bone from its socket and discard the bone. Take care not to pierce the skin. Repeat with the remaining wings.

Soak the vermicelli in boiling water for 7 minutes. Drain and cut into 2 cm (3/4 inch) pieces with scissors.

Put the palm sugar and fish sauce in a small bowl and stir until the sugar has dissolved.

Combine the pork, spring onion, garlic, chilli and the fish sauce mixture in a food processor and process to combine. Transfer to a bowl, then stir in the coriander and vermicelli. Divide the mixture into 12 even-sized balls. Stuff each boned-out section of chicken wing with a ball of mixture and secure firmly with a toothpick.

Put the wings in a bamboo or metal steamer. Cover and steam over a wok of simmering water for 8 minutes. Remove the wings from the steamer, then set aside to firm and cool.

Fill a wok or large saucepan one-third full of oil and heat to 180°C (350°F), or until a cube of bread dropped into the oil browns in 15 seconds. Coat the wings in the seasoned flour. Deep-fry the chicken wings, in batches, until golden brown and cooked through. Drain on paper towel, then remove the toothpicks. Serve with the chilli sauce.

PREPARATION TIME: 30 MINUTES COOKING TIME: 20 MINUTES

SPICED PRAWN PAKORAS

16 raw prawns (shrimp)
85 g (3 oz/¾ cup) besan (chickpea flour)
½ teaspoon baking powder
¼ teaspoon ground turmeric
1 teaspoon ground coriander
½ teaspoon ground cumin
½ teaspoon chilli powder
oil, for deep-frying
1 tablespoon egg white

DIPPING SAUCE
250 g (9 oz/1 cup) plain yoghurt
3 tablespoons chopped coriander
(cilantro) leaves
1 teaspoon ground cumin
garam masala, to sprinkle

MAKES 16

Peel the prawns and gently pull out the dark vein from each prawn back, starting from the head end, leaving the tails intact.

Sift the besan, baking powder and spices into a large bowl and season with a little salt. Make a well in the centre and gradually add 250 ml (9 fl oz/1 cup) water and stir gently until combined. Beat the egg white until firm peaks form and then fold into the batter.

Fill a wok one-third full of oil and heat to 180°C (350°F), or until a cube of bread dropped into the oil browns in 15 seconds. Using the tail as a handle, dip the prawns into the batter, then lower gently into the oil. Deep-fry the prawns in batches, until the batter is lightly golden; it won't become really crisp. Drain on crumpled paper towel.

To make the dipping sauce, combine the yoghurt, coriander and cumin. Sprinkle with the garam masala. Serve with the prawn pakoras.

PREPARATION TIME: 20 MINUTES   COOKING TIME: 10 MINUTES

THAI CHICKEN ROLLS

600 g (1 lb 5 oz) minced (ground) chicken
4 lemon grass stems, white part only, finely chopped
4 red chillies, seeded and finely chopped
6 red Asian shallots, finely chopped
2 tablespoons chopped Vietnamese mint
3 tablespoons finely chopped coriander (cilantro) leaves
2 tablespoons fish sauce
2 tablespoons lime juice
100 g (3½ oz) packet tofu skins
oil, for deep-frying
4 makrut (kaffir lime) leaves, finely shredded, to garnish

MAKES 30

Put the chicken, lemon grass, chilli, shallots, mint, coriander, fish sauce and lime juice in a food processor and process to combine.

Cut thirty 10 x 16 cm (4 x 6¼ inch) rectangles from the tofu skins. Brush the tofu skin lightly with water to soften it for rolling. Roll 1 tablespoon of the chicken mixture into a log and place on each tofu rectangle. Roll up from the short end, folding in the ends as you roll.

Fill a wok or deep heavy-based saucepan one-third full of oil and heat to 180°C (350°F), or until a cube of bread dropped into the oil browns in 15 seconds. Deep-fry the chicken rolls in batches for 1 minute, or until golden brown. If the tofu skin is browning before the chicken is cooked, turn the heat down. Drain well on crumpled paper towel. Serve garnished with finely shredded makrut leaves.

PREPARATION TIME: 25 MINUTES   COOKING TIME: 10 MINUTES

KOREAN POTATO FRITTERS

DIPPING SAUCE
2 spring onions (scallions), finely chopped
1 small garlic clove, finely chopped
1½ tablespoons Japanese soy sauce
1 tablespoon mirin
2 teaspoons sesame seeds, toasted and ground
1 teaspoon sugar
drizzle of sesame oil
¼ teaspoon chilli flakes (optional)

POTATO FRITTERS
500 g (1 lb 2 oz) potatoes
5 spring onions (scallions), shredded
2 eggs, lightly beaten
2 tablespoons cornflour (cornstarch)
peanut oil, for deep-frying

MAKES 12

To make the dipping sauce, combine all the ingredients in a small non-metallic bowl. Set aside.

To make the potato fritters, peel and coarsely grate the potatoes into a large non-metallic bowl. Cover with cold water to prevent discolouration and set aside for 10 minutes. Drain and squeeze out any excess moisture with your hands. Put in a clean bowl with the shredded spring onions and mix well.

In a separate small bowl, combine the eggs and cornflour and season with pepper. Pour over the potato mixture and mix well. Mould handfuls of batter with the palms of your hands, gently flattening them out into patties with a 5 cm (2 inch) diameter.

Fill a wok or deep heavy-based saucepan one-third full of oil and heat to 180°C (350°F), or until a cube of bread dropped into the oil browns in 15 seconds. Carefully drop the fritters into the oil, in batches, and cook, turning once, for 5 minutes, or until golden. Remove and drain on crumpled paper towel. Serve immediately with the dipping sauce.

PREPARATION TIME: 15 MINUTES +   COOKING TIME: 20 MINUTES

DEEP-FRIED CHICKEN BALLS

50 g (1¾ oz) dried rice vermicelli
500 g (1 lb 2 oz) minced (ground) chicken
3 garlic cloves, finely chopped
1 tablespoon chopped fresh ginger
1 red chilli, seeded and finely chopped
1 egg, lightly beaten
2 spring onions (scallions), thinly sliced
4 tablespoons chopped coriander
(cilantro) leaves
40 g (1½ oz/⅓ cup) plain (all-purpose)
flour
60 g (2¼ oz/⅓ cup) tinned water
chestnuts, finely chopped
oil, for deep-frying

DIPPING SAUCE
125 ml (4 fl oz/½ cup) sweet chilli sauce
125 ml (4 fl oz/½ cup) soy sauce
1 tablespoon Chinese rice wine

MAKES ABOUT 30

Cover the vermicelli with boiling water and soak for 6–7 minutes. Drain, then cut into short lengths with scissors.

Combine the chicken, garlic, ginger, chilli, egg, spring onion, coriander, flour and water chestnuts in a large bowl. Mix in the vermicelli and season with salt. Refrigerate for 30 minutes. Roll heaped tablespoons of the chilled mixture into balls.

Fill a wok or deep heavy-based saucepan one-third full of oil and heat to 180°C (350°F), or until a cube of bread dropped into the oil browns in 15 seconds. Deep-fry the balls in batches for 2 minutes, or until golden brown and cooked through. Drain on crumpled paper towel.

To make the dipping sauce, combine the sweet chilli sauce, soy sauce and rice wine. Serve with the hot chicken balls.

PREPARATION TIME: 20 MINUTES +   COOKING TIME: 15 MINUTES

CRISPY LAMB WITH LETTUCE

400 g (14 oz) lamb backstraps or loin fillets
2 tablespoons light soy sauce
1 tablespoon Chinese rice wine
2 teaspoons fish sauce
½ teaspoon sesame oil
2 garlic cloves, crushed
1 teaspoon finely grated fresh ginger
40 g (1½ oz/⅓ cup) cornflour (cornstarch)
oil, for deep-frying
12 baby cos lettuce leaves
plum sauce, to serve
4 spring onions (scallions), thinly sliced, to serve

SERVES 4

Wrap the lamb in plastic wrap and put it in the freezer for 30 minutes, or until semi-frozen. Remove the plastic wrap and cut the lamb lengthways into three thin slices, then thinly slice across the grain, so that you have julienne strips. Place in a bowl with the soy sauce, rice wine, fish sauce, sesame oil, garlic and ginger. Mix well to coat, then cover and refrigerate for 2 hours.

Sift the cornflour over the lamb and mix well. Spread the lamb out on a tray and return to the refrigerator, uncovered, for 1 hour.

Preheat the oven to 150°C (300°F/Gas 2). Heat the oil in a wok or deep heavy-based saucepan to 180°C (350°F), or until a cube of bread dropped into the oil browns in 15 seconds. Deep-fry the lamb in batches for 5–6 minutes, or until crisp and browned. Lift the lamb out with a slotted spoon and drain on crumpled paper towel. Keep warm in the oven while you cook the remainder.

To serve, cup a lettuce leaf in your hand. With the other hand, drizzle the inside with a little plum sauce, fill with the lamb mixture and sprinkle with spring onion. Alternatively, arrange the lettuce, lamb, spring onion and plum sauce in separate dishes for your guests to assemble their own 'cups'.

PREPARATION TIME: 15 MINUTES + COOKING TIME: 20 MINUTES

CHICKEN AND MUSHROOM
RICE PAPER PARCELS

1–2 tablespoons Chinese barbecue sauce

1 tablespoon Chinese rice wine

2 teaspoons hoisin sauce

2 teaspoons light soy sauce

½ teaspoon sesame oil

pinch Chinese five-spice

pinch white pepper

2 teaspoons grated fresh ginger

2 spring onions (scallions), finely chopped, white and green parts separated

400 g (14 oz) boneless, skinless chicken breast, thinly sliced

4 dried shiitake mushrooms

60 ml (2 fl oz/¼ cup) vegetable oil

125 g (4½ oz) tinned bamboo shoots, rinsed, drained and finely sliced

12 snow peas (mangetout), shredded

2 garlic cloves, finely chopped

24 square rice paper wrappers

hoisin sauce, for dipping (optional)

oil, for deep-frying

MAKES 24

Combine the Chinese barbecue sauce, rice wine, hoisin sauce, soy sauce, sesame oil, five-spice, white pepper, 1 teaspoon of the ginger and the white part of the spring onion in a non-metallic bowl. Add the chicken and stir to coat in the marinade. Cover and refrigerate for at least 2 hours.

Meanwhile, put the shiitake mushrooms in a heatproof bowl, cover with boiling water and soak for 20 minutes. Squeeze the mushrooms dry, discard the stems and thinly slice the caps.

Heat a wok over high heat, add 1 tablespoon of the oil and swirl to coat the base and side. Add the mushrooms, bamboo shoots and snow peas and stir-fry for 1–2 minutes. Add another tablespoon of oil, the garlic and remaining ginger and stir-fry for 30 seconds. Transfer to a non-metallic bowl.

Heat another tablespoon of the oil in the wok, add the drained chicken and stir-fry for 2–3 minutes, or until the chicken is cooked. Transfer to the bowl with the vegetables. Add the green part of the spring onion to the bowl. Mix well, then set aside to cool for 15 minutes.

Take a rice paper wrapper and place it diagonally on the work surface, so the bottom corner of the diamond is closest to you. Using 1 tablespoon of the chicken mixture, roll it into a sausage shape and lay it vertically in the middle of the wrapper. Fold up the wrapper like an envelope, tucking in the edges. Repeat with the remaining wrappers and filling.

Fill a wok or deep heavy-based saucepan one-third full of oil and heat to 180°C (350°F), or until a cube of bread dropped into the oil browns in 15 seconds. Working in batches, gently lower four to six chicken parcels into the oil and deep-fry for 1–2 minutes, turning halfway through cooking to ensure both sides are evenly browned and crisp, and that the filling is cooked through. Drain well on crumpled paper towel and serve immediately with some hoisin sauce for dipping, if desired.

PREPARATION TIME: 30 MINUTES +   COOKING TIME: 20 MINUTES

MERMAID'S TRESSES

350 g (12 oz) bok choy (pak choy)
or choy sum
peanut oil, for deep-frying
caster (superfine) sugar, to sprinkle

SERVES 4

Very finely shred the leaves of the bok choy or choy sum and dry with paper towel.

Fill a wok or deep heavy-based saucepan one-third full of the oil and heat to 180°C (350°F), or until a cube of bread dropped into the oil browns in 15 seconds. Deep-fry the bok choy shreds, a handful at a time, for about 20 seconds, or until they stop sizzling and darken — they burn easily, so be careful. Drain on crumpled paper towel. To serve, sprinkle with the sugar and some salt.

PREPARATION TIME: 10 MINUTES   COOKING TIME: 5 MINUTES

NOTE: These are a popular snack in China. Alternatively, they can be used as a garnish.

CRISPY VERMICELLI CAKES WITH SESAME VEGETABLES

400 g (14 oz) dried rice vermicelli
oil, for shallow-frying
2 teaspoons sesame oil
2 carrots, cut into matchsticks
1 red capsicum (pepper), seeded, membrane removed and cut into matchsticks
2 zucchini (courgettes), cut into matchsticks
4 spring onions (scallions), cut into matchsticks
½–1 tablespoon oyster sauce

MAKES 12

Cover the vermicelli with boiling water and soak for 3 minutes, then drain thoroughly until very dry.

Heat the oil in a large heavy-based frying pan over medium heat. Shape tablespoons of the noodles into flat discs and shallow-fry them in batches for 3 minutes, or until crisp and golden. Drain on crumpled paper towel.

Heat the sesame oil in a wok over medium heat and swirl to coat the base and side. Add the vegetables and stir-fry for 3 minutes until softened slightly. Stir in the oyster sauce and cook for a further 2 minutes. Serve the vermicelli cakes topped with the vegetables.

PREPARATION TIME: 20 MINUTES   COOKING TIME: 15 MINUTES

VEGETABLE TEMPURA PATTIES

WASABI MAYONNAISE
125 g (4½ oz/½ cup) whole-egg mayonnaise
2 teaspoons wasabi paste
1 teaspoon Japanese soy sauce
1 teaspoon sake

1 small zucchini (courgette), grated
1 small potato, cut into matchsticks
½ carrot, cut into matchsticks
½ onion, thinly sliced
100 g (3½ oz) orange sweet potato, grated
4 spring onions (scallions), cut into 2 cm (¾ inch) lengths
4 nori sheets, shredded
250 g (9 oz/2 cups) tempura flour, sifted
500 ml (17 fl oz/2 cups) chilled soda water
oil, for deep-frying
2 tablespoons shredded pickled ginger, to serve

SERVES 4

To make the wasabi mayonnaise, combine the ingredients in a small bowl. Keep refrigerated until ready to serve.

To make the patties, put the zucchini, potato, carrot, onion, sweet potato, spring onion and nori in a bowl. Toss together.

Sift the tempura flour into a large bowl and make a well in the centre. Add the soda water and loosely mix together with chopsticks or a fork until just combined — the batter should still be lumpy. Add the vegetables and quickly fold through to coat.

Fill a wok or large heavy-based saucepan one-third full of oil and heat to 180°C (350°F), or until a cube of bread dropped into the oil browns in 15 seconds. Gently drop 60 g (2¼ oz/¼ cup) of the vegetable mixture into the oil, making sure that the patty is not too compact, and cook for 1–2 minutes, or until golden and crisp. Drain on crumpled paper towel. Repeat with the remaining mixture.

Season with sea salt and serve immediately with the wasabi mayonnaise and the pickled ginger.

PREPARATION TIME: 25 MINUTES   COOKING TIME: 15 MINUTES

PRAWN TOASTS

DIPPING SAUCE
125 ml (4 fl oz/½ cup) tomato sauce (ketchup)
2 garlic cloves, crushed
2 small red chillies, seeded and finely chopped
2 tablespoons hoisin sauce
2 teaspoons worcestershire sauce

350 g (12 oz) raw prawns (shrimp)
1 garlic clove
75 g (2½ oz) tinned water chestnuts, drained
1 tablespoon chopped coriander (cilantro) leaves
2 cm (¾ inch) piece ginger, roughly chopped
2 eggs, separated
¼ teaspoon white pepper
12 slices white bread, crusts removed
155 g (5½ oz/1 cup) sesame seeds
oil, for deep-frying

MAKES 36

To make the dipping sauce, combine the tomato sauce, garlic, chillies, hoisin sauce and worcestershire sauce in a small bowl. Set aside until ready to serve.

Peel the prawns and gently pull out the dark vein from each prawn back, starting from the head end. Put the prawns in a food processor with the garlic, water chestnuts, coriander, ginger, egg whites, white pepper and ¼ teaspoon salt and process for 20–30 seconds, or until smooth.

Brush the top of each slice of bread with lightly beaten egg yolk, then spread evenly with the prawn mixture. Sprinkle generously with sesame seeds, pressing them down gently. Cut each slice of bread into three even strips.

Fill a wok or deep heavy-based saucepan one-third full of oil and heat to 180°C (350°F), or until a cube of bread dropped into the oil browns in 15 seconds. Starting with the prawn mixture face down, deep-fry the toasts in small batches for 10–15 seconds, or until golden and crisp, turning the toasts over halfway through. Remove with tongs or a slotted spoon and drain on crumpled paper towel. Serve with the dipping sauce.

PREPARATION TIME: 20 MINUTES   COOKING TIME: 15 MINUTES

COCONUT PRAWNS WITH CHILLI DRESSING

24 large raw prawns (shrimp)

plain (all-purpose) flour, to coat

1 egg

1 tablespoon milk

60 g (2¼ oz/1 cup) shredded coconut

1 handful coriander (cilantro) leaves, chopped

2½ tablespoons vegetable oil

300 g (10½ oz) red Asian shallots, chopped

2 garlic cloves, finely chopped

2 teaspoons finely chopped fresh ginger

1 red chilli, seeded and thinly sliced

1 teaspoon ground turmeric

270 ml (9½ fl oz) tinned coconut cream

2 makrut (kaffir lime) leaves, thinly sliced

2 teaspoons lime juice

2 teaspoons grated palm sugar (jaggery)

3 teaspoons fish sauce

oil, for deep-frying

1 tablespoon chopped coriander (cilantro) leaves, extra

SERVES 4

Peel the prawns and gently pull out the dark vein from each prawn back, starting from the head end. Holding the prawns by their tails, coat them in flour, then dip them into the combined egg and milk, and then in the combined coconut and coriander. Refrigerate for 30 minutes.

To make the chilli dressing, heat the oil in a saucepan and cook the shallots, garlic, ginger, chilli and turmeric over medium heat for 3–5 minutes, or until fragrant. Add the coconut cream, makrut leaves, lime juice, palm sugar and fish sauce. Bring to the boil, then reduce the heat and simmer for 2–3 minutes, or until thick. Keep warm.

Fill a wok or deep heavy-based saucepan one-third full of oil and heat to 180°C (350°F), or until a cube of bread dropped into the oil browns in 15 seconds. Holding the prawns by their tails, gently lower them into the wok and cook in batches for 3–5 minutes, or until golden. Drain on crumpled paper towel and season with salt.

Add the extra coriander to the chilli dressing and serve with the prawns.

PREPARATION TIME: 35 MINUTES +   COOKING TIME: 30 MINUTES

CHICKEN KARAAGE

1.5 kg (3 lb 5 oz) chicken
125 ml (4 fl oz/½ cup) Japanese soy sauce
60 ml (2 fl oz/¼ cup) mirin
2 tablespoons sake
1 tablespoon finely chopped fresh ginger
4 garlic cloves, crushed
oil, for deep-frying
cornflour (cornstarch), to coat
lemon wedges, to serve

MAKES 20 PIECES

Using a cleaver or a large kitchen knife, remove the wings from the chicken and chop them in half across the joint. Cut the chicken into 16 even-sized pieces by cutting it in half down the centre, then across each half to form four even pieces. Cut each quarter into four pieces, trying to retain some skin on each piece. You should have 20 pieces in total, including the four wing pieces.

Combine the soy sauce, mirin, sake, ginger and garlic in a large non-metallic bowl. Add the chicken and toss to coat well. Cover and refrigerate overnight, turning occasionally to evenly coat the chicken in the marinade.

Preheat the oven to 150°C (300°F/Gas 2). Fill a wok or deep heavy-based saucepan one-third full with oil and heat to 180°C (350°F), or until a cube of bread dropped into the oil browns in 15 seconds. While the oil is heating, drain the chicken and coat thoroughly in well-seasoned cornflour, shaking lightly to remove any excess.

Deep-fry the chicken, in batches, for 4–5 minutes, or until crisp and golden and the chicken is just cooked through and tender. Drain well on crumpled paper towel. Keep the cooked chicken warm in the oven while you cook the remainder. Serve hot with lemon wedges.

PREPARATION TIME: 20 MINUTES +   COOKING TIME: 30 MINUTES

THAI RICE CRACKERS WITH DIPS

370 g (13 oz) long-grain or jasmine rice, cooked

oil, for deep-frying

CHILLI JAM

3 tablespoons dried shrimp

500 ml (17 fl oz/2 cups) oil

220 g (7¾ oz/2 cups) sliced red Asian shallots

35 garlic cloves, thinly sliced

4-5 long red chillies, seeded and finely chopped

70 g (3¼ oz/½ cup) grated light palm sugar (jaggery)

3 tablespoons tamarind syrup

2 tablespoons fish sauce

TAMARIND AND PORK DIP

2 teaspoons shrimp paste

3 garlic cloves, roughly chopped

1 small red chilli, roughly chopped

2 teaspoons grated fresh ginger

1 tablespoon finely chopped spring onion (scallion)

1-2 tablespoons tamarind concentrate

100 g (3½ oz) lean minced (ground) pork

100 g (3½ oz) raw prawn (shrimp) meat

4 tablespoons finely chopped coriander (cilantro) leaves

1 tablespoon peanut oil

125 ml (4 fl oz/½ cup) coconut milk

1 tablespoon fish sauce

1 tablespoon grated light palm sugar (jaggery)

1 tablespoon lime juice

2 tablespoons chopped coriander (cilantro) leaves

SERVES 8-10

Preheat the oven to 140°C (275°F/Gas 1) and lightly grease a flat baking tray with oil. Spread the cooked, cooled rice over the bottom of the tray. Using wet hands to prevent the rice from sticking, spread the rice to a thickness of about two or three grains. Use a knife to score a grid in the rice, forming 4 cm (1½ inch) squares. Put the tray of rice in the oven and bake for 1 hour, or until the rice is completely dry. When cool enough to handle, break the rice along the scored lines.

To make the chilli jam, soak the dried shrimp in hot water for 5 minutes, drain well, then dry and roughly chop. Heat the oil in a saucepan over medium–high heat, add the shallots and garlic and cook for 10 minutes, stirring constantly, until golden. Add the shrimp and chillies and cook for 5 minutes, stirring constantly. Remove from the heat. Drain and reserve the oil. Put the fried mixture in a food processor and blend, gradually adding 60 ml (2 fl oz/¼ cup) of the reserved cooking oil to form a paste. Put the mixture in a saucepan over medium heat and when it begins to simmer add the palm sugar, tamarind syrup and fish sauce. Cook for 5 minutes, stirring frequently, until it thickens. Cool before serving.

To make the tamarind and pork dip, wrap the shrimp paste in foil and put under a hot grill (broiler) for 2-3 minutes. Put the garlic, chilli, ginger, spring onion, tamarind concentrate, shrimp paste and 1 teaspoon salt in a small food processor and combine to form a smooth paste. Combine the pork, prawn meat and finely chopped coriander in a bowl. Heat the peanut oil in a frying pan over medium heat and add the tamarind paste mixture. Cook for 2-3 minutes, or until fragrant. Add the pork and prawn mixture, stir well and cook for a further 2-3 minutes, or until browned, stirring constantly. Pour in the coconut milk and cook over medium heat for 5 minutes, or until the liquid is absorbed and the meat is cooked through, stirring constantly to prevent the mixture from sticking to the bottom of the pan. Remove from the heat, then stir in the fish sauce, palm sugar, lime juice and coriander leaves. Best served warm.

To cook the rice squares, heat the oil in a wok or deep heavy-based saucepan over high heat to 180°C (350°F), or until a cube of bread dropped into the oil browns in 15 seconds. Drop the rice squares into the oil, in batches, and cook for 1-2 minutes, or until golden. Remove and drain on paper towel. Serve immediately with the chilli jam and tamarind and pork dip.

PREPARATION TIME: 40 MINUTES +   COOKING TIME: 2 HOURS

SALT AND PEPPER TOFU PUFFS

125 ml (4 fl oz/½ cup) sweet chilli sauce

2 tablespoons lemon juice

250 g (9 oz/2 cups) cornflour (cornstarch)

1 tablespoon ground white pepper

2 teaspoons caster (superfine) sugar

380 g (13½ oz) fried tofu puffs, halved and patted dry

4 egg whites, lightly beaten

peanut oil, for deep-frying

lemon wedges, to serve

SERVES 4–6

Combine the sweet chilli sauce and lemon juice in a bowl and set aside.

Put the cornflour, 2 tablespoons salt, white pepper and sugar in a large bowl and mix together well. Dip the tofu puffs into the egg white, then toss in the cornflour mixture, shaking off any excess.

Fill a wok or deep heavy-based saucepan one-third full of oil and heat to 180°C (350°F), or until a cube of bread dropped into the oil browns in 15 seconds. Cook the tofu puffs in batches for 1–2 minutes, or until crisp. Drain on crumpled paper towel. Serve immediately with the sweet chilli sauce mixture and lemon wedges.

PREPARATION TIME: 15 MINUTES   COOKING TIME: 10 MINUTES

PRAWNS IN RICE PAPER

20 rice paper wrappers

350 g (12 oz) raw prawn (shrimp) meat

4 cm (1½ inch) piece fresh ginger, grated

2 garlic cloves, crushed

3 spring onions (scallions), finely chopped

1 tablespoon rice flour

1 egg white, beaten

2 teaspoons sesame oil

2 tablespoons cornflour (cornstarch)

oil, for deep-frying

2 tablespoons sesame seeds, toasted

plum sauce, to serve (optional)

MAKES 20

Place four rice paper wrappers on the work surface. Brush generously with water, then leave for 2 minutes, or until soft and pliable. Gently transfer to a plate. (They may be stacked on top of each other at this stage.) Repeat the brushing with the remaining wrappers, then cover with plastic wrap.

Finely chop the prawn meat and combine with the ginger, garlic, spring onion, rice flour, egg white and sesame oil. Use your fingertips to combine. Blend the cornflour with 2 tablespoons water in a small bowl.

Working with one wrapper at a time, spread 1 tablespoon of prawn mixture on the wrapper. Fold up the bottom section to encase the filling. Roll the wrapper over once, lightly pushing down to flatten out the filling. Fold in the sides and brush the edges with the cornflour mixture, then wrap to form a parcel. Repeat with the remaining wrappers and filling.

Fill a wok or deep heavy-based saucepan one-third full of oil and heat to 180°C (350°F), or until a cube of bread dropped into the oil browns in 15 seconds. Add several parcels and deep-fry for 4–5 minutes, or until golden brown. Remove with a slotted spoon or tongs, drain on crumpled paper towel and repeat with the remainder. Sprinkle with sesame seeds and serve with plum sauce, if desired.

PREPARATION TIME: 35 MINUTES   COOKING TIME: 5–10 MINUTES

Salt and pepper tofu puffs

PORK AND LEMON GRASS WON TONS

400 g (14 oz) minced (ground) pork
1 teaspoon finely chopped fresh ginger
1 lemon grass stem, white part only, finely sliced
230 g (8 oz) tinned water chestnuts, drained and finely chopped
2 tablespoons finely chopped garlic chives
½ teaspoon chilli paste
2 tablespoons plum sauce
1 teaspoon chilli oil
1 teaspoon sesame oil
1 tablespoon cornflour (cornstarch)
56 square won ton wrappers
oil, for deep-frying

DIPPING SAUCE
125 ml (4 fl oz/½ cup) light soy sauce
60 ml (2 fl oz/¼ cup) balsamic vinegar
1 teaspoon finely grated fresh ginger
1 teaspoon chilli oil

MAKES 56

Put the pork, ginger, lemon grass, water chestnuts, garlic chives, chilli paste, plum sauce, chilli oil, sesame oil and cornflour in a bowl. Mix with your hands. Cover, then refrigerate for 1 hour.

To make the dipping sauce, combine the ingredients in a jar with a lid and shake to combine. Refrigerate until needed.

Work with one wrapper at a time, keeping the rest covered. Spoon 2 teaspoons of the pork filling into the centre of the wrapper and lightly brush the edges with water. Gather up the corners, bring them together in the centre and press firmly to seal. Repeat with the remaining wrappers and filling.

Fill a wok or deep heavy-based saucepan one-third full of oil and heat to 180°C (350°F), or until a cube of bread dropped into the oil browns in 15 seconds. Deep-fry the won tons in batches for 3–4 minutes, or until lightly browned. Remove with a slotted spoon, drain on crumpled paper towel and serve hot with the dipping sauce.

PREPARATION TIME: 40 MINUTES +   COOKING TIME: 20 MINUTES

CRISPY VEGETABLES IN TOFU

4 large dried shiitake mushrooms
2 tablespoons peanut oil
1 teaspoon grated fresh ginger
2 spring onions (scallions), thinly sliced
1 small carrot, cut into matchsticks
100 g (3½ oz) tinned bamboo shoots, cut
into matchsticks
50 g (1¾ oz) firm tofu, finely chopped
1 tablespoon light soy sauce
½ teaspoon sugar
2 teaspoons cornflour (cornstarch)
six 20 x 25 cm (8 x 10 inch) tofu sheets
peanut oil, for deep-frying

MAKES 6

Put the shiitake mushrooms in a heatproof bowl, cover with boiling water and soak for 20 minutes. Squeeze the mushrooms dry, discard the stems and finely chop the caps.

To make the filling, heat a wok over high heat, add the oil and swirl to coat the base and side. Add the mushrooms, ginger, spring onion, carrot, bamboo shoots and tofu and stir-fry over medium–high heat for 1 minute. Add the soy sauce, sugar and ½ teaspoon salt and cook for a further minute, tossing all the ingredients together. Transfer to a colander sitting over a bowl and allow to drain and cool.

Combine the cornflour with 1 tablespoon water to form a paste. Soak the tofu sheets in lukewarm water for 10–15 seconds to soften, then drain well and pat dry with paper towel.

Lay a tofu sheet on a work surface and brush the edges with the cornflour paste. Place 2 tablespoons of filling at one end of the sheet, then fold the edges over towards the centre and roll up to form a neat rectangular parcel. Repeat with the remaining sheets and filling to make six large rolls. Refrigerate for at least 30 minutes, or until ready to use.

Fill a wok or deep heavy-based saucepan one-third full of peanut oil and heat to 180°C (350°F), or until a cube of bread dropped into the oil browns in 15 seconds. Deep-fry the rolls in batches for 2–3 minutes, or until crisp and golden. Drain on crumpled paper towel and serve.

PREPARATION TIME: 20 MINUTES +   COOKING TIME: 10 MINUTES

SESAME PRAWNS WITH TANGY MINT CHUTNEY

24 raw king prawns (shrimp)
30 g (1 oz/¼ cup) plain (all-purpose) flour
1 egg, lightly beaten
65 g (2¼ oz/⅔ cup) dry breadcrumbs
80 g (2¾ oz/½ cup) sesame seeds
oil, for deep-frying

TANGY MINT CHUTNEY
1 small handful mint leaves
140 g (5 oz/½ cup) fruit chutney
2 tablespoons lemon juice

MAKES 24

Peel the prawns, leaving the tails intact. Carefully cut the prawns down the back, pull out the dark vein, starting from the head end. Flatten the prawns slightly. Toss the prawns in the flour and shake off the excess. Dip the floured prawns in the beaten egg and coat with the combined breadcrumbs and sesame seeds.

Fill a wok or deep heavy-based saucepan one-third full of oil and heat to 180°C (350°F), or until a cube of bread dropped into the oil browns in 15 seconds. Deep-fry the prawns in batches for about 2 minutes, or until golden brown. Remove from the oil with tongs or a slotted spoon. Drain on crumpled paper towel.

To make the tangy mint chutney, combine the mint, chutney and lemon juice in a blender or food processor and blend for 15 seconds, or until smooth. Serve as a dip with the hot prawns.

PREPARATION TIME: 20 MINUTES   COOKING TIME: 15 MINUTES

NOTE: The prawns can be crumbed a day ahead. Place in a single layer on a tray, cover and refrigerate. Alternatively, freeze in a single layer and when frozen, place in a plastic bag and seal. Thaw in a single layer on a baking tray in the refrigerator before cooking.

PORK AND NOODLE BALLS
WITH SWEET CHILLI SAUCE

DIPPING SAUCE
80 ml (2½ fl oz/⅓ cup) sweet chilli sauce
2 teaspoons mirin
2 teaspoons finely chopped fresh ginger
125 ml (4 fl oz/½ cup) Japanese soy sauce

250 g (9 oz) hokkien (egg) noodles
300 g (10½ oz) minced (ground) pork
6 spring onions (scallions), finely chopped
2 garlic cloves, crushed
4 tablespoons finely chopped coriander
(cilantro) leaves
1 tablespoon fish sauce
2 tablespoons oyster sauce
1½ tablespoons lime juice
peanut oil, for deep-frying

MAKES 30

To make the dipping sauce, combine the sweet chilli sauce, mirin, ginger and Japanese soy sauce in a bowl. Set aside.

Place the noodles in a bowl and cover with boiling water. Soak for about 1 minute, or until tender. Drain very well and pat dry with paper towel. Cut the noodles into 5 cm (2 inch) lengths, then transfer to a large bowl. Add the pork, spring onion, garlic, coriander, fish sauce, oyster sauce and lime juice and combine the mixture well using your hands, making sure the pork is evenly distributed.

Using a tablespoon of mixture at a time, roll each spoonful into a ball to make 30 in total, shaping and pressing each ball firmly with your hands to ensure they remain intact.

Fill a wok or deep heavy-based saucepan one-third full of oil and heat to 180°C (350°F), or until a cube of bread dropped into the oil browns in 15 seconds. Deep-fry the pork balls in batches for 2–3 minutes, or until golden and cooked through. Drain on crumpled paper towel. Serve hot with the dipping sauce.

PREPARATION TIME: 30 MINUTES   COOKING TIME: 15 MINUTES

CRUSTED TUNA CRISPS

WASABI CREAM
60 ml (2 fl oz/¼ cup) pouring (whipping) cream
2 tablespoons sour cream
1 tablespoon wasabi powder
½ tablespoon lemon juice
1 tablespoon rice wine vinegar
½ teaspoon sugar

12 round gow gee wrappers
oil, for deep-frying, plus extra
500 g (1 lb 2 oz) tuna steaks, 2.5 cm (1 inch) thick
80 g (2¾ oz/½ cup) sesame seeds

SALAD
125 g (4½ oz) watercress
1 Lebanese (short) cucumber
3 radishes
1 teaspoon grated fresh ginger
3 teaspoons rice wine vinegar
1 tablespoon sesame oil
1 tablespoon peanut or corn oil

MAKES 24

To make the wasabi cream, whisk the cream until it thickens, then gently stir in the sour cream, wasabi powder, lemon juice, rice wine vinegar and sugar. Season to taste. Refrigerate for at least 30 minutes.

Cut each gow gee wrapper in half. Fill a wok or deep heavy-based saucepan one-third full of oil and heat to 180°C (350°F), or until a cube of bread dropped into the oil browns in 15 seconds. Fry the gow gee wrappers in batches for 30 seconds each side, or until slightly brown and crisp. Drain on crumpled paper towel.

Cut the tuna steaks into 4 cm (1½ inch) wide strips. Lightly brush with 2 teaspoons of oil, season and toss in the sesame seeds. Refrigerate.

Break the watercress into small sprigs. Use a vegetable peeler to slice the cucumber into thin strips. Rotate the cucumber and stop when you get to the seeds. Use the peeler to slice the radishes into thin pieces. Combine the cucumber, radish and watercress and set aside.

Combine the ginger, rice wine vinegar, sesame oil and peanut oil in a small non-metallic bowl. Season and set aside.

Heat 1 tablespoon oil in a wok or heavy-based saucepan over medium heat. Sear the tuna on all sides for 1 minute each side. The sesame seeds should be golden brown and the centre of the tuna pink. Slice the tuna crossways into 24 pieces.

When ready to serve, stir the ginger dressing. Pour over the watercress, cucumber and radish and toss to combine. Place a small pile of salad on the wrappers, followed by a piece of tuna and some wasabi cream. Serve at room temperature.

PREPARATION TIME: 45 MINUTES +   COOKING TIME: 15 MINUTES

PRAWN PARCELS

1 tablespoon oil
2 garlic cloves, crushed
1 tablespoon grated fresh ginger
2 spring onions (scallions), chopped
500 g (1 lb 2 oz) raw prawns (shrimp),
peeled and chopped
½ teaspoon fish sauce
½ teaspoon sugar
1 tablespoon lemon juice
2 tablespoons chopped coriander
(cilantro) leaves
6 large spring roll wrappers, quartered
oil, for deep-frying
chives, for tying
sweet chilli sauce, to serve

MAKES 24

Heat the oil in a frying pan, add the garlic and ginger and cook over low heat for 2 minutes. Add the spring onion and cook for 2 minutes. Increase the heat to high, add the prawns and stir-fry for 2 minutes, or until the colour just changes. Be careful not to overcook the prawns or they will become tough once deep-fried. Add the fish sauce, sugar, lemon juice and coriander to the pan. Toss with the prawns for 1 minute. Remove from the heat and allow to cool slightly.

Divide the cooled mixture into 24 portions. Place one portion in the centre of each piece of spring roll wrapper. Brush the edges with water and fold to form a parcel.

Fill a wok or deep heavy-based saucepan one-third full of oil and heat to 180°C (350°F), or until a cube of bread dropped into the oil browns in 15 seconds. Deep-fry the parcels one at a time, holding them with tongs for the first few seconds to keep them intact. Cook for 3–4 minutes, or until golden brown. Drain on crumpled paper towel. Tie with lengths of chives and serve with sweet chilli sauce.

PREPARATION TIME: 30 MINUTES   COOKING TIME: 20 MINUTES

NOTE: If the spring roll wrappers are very thin, you may need to use two together.

FRIED SPICY TEMPEH

4 small red chillies
2 lemon grass stems, white part only
2 makrut (kaffir lime) leaves
125 ml (4 fl oz/½ cup) oil
10 red Asian shallots, finely sliced
2 large garlic cloves, finely chopped
500 g (1 lb 2 oz) tempeh, sliced into matchsticks
4 cm (1½ inch) piece fresh galangal, peeled and thinly sliced
3 teaspoons tamarind purée
60 g (2¼ oz/⅓ cup) chopped palm sugar (jaggery) or soft brown sugar
steamed rice, to serve

SERVES 4–6

Split the chillies lengthways and remove the seeds and membrane. Finely slice the chillies diagonally. Bruise the lemon grass and makrut leaves with the back of a large knife.

Heat 2 tablespoons of the oil in a wok or frying pan and fry the shallots and garlic in batches over medium-low heat for 2–3 minutes, or until crisp. Drain on crumpled paper towel. Heat the remaining oil and fry the tempeh in batches for 3–4 minutes, or until very crisp (you may need to add a little more oil). Drain on crumpled paper towel. Discard all the oil except 2 teaspoons.

Heat the reserved oil in the wok and add the chilli, lemon grass, makrut leaves and galangal. Cook over medium heat for 2 minutes, or until fragrant. Add the tamarind purée, palm sugar, 1 teaspoon salt and 1 tablespoon water. Cook for 2–3 minutes, or until the sauce is thick and has caramelized. Add the crispy shallots, garlic and tempeh and stir-fry for 1–2 minutes, or until all the liquid has evaporated. Turn off the heat, spread the mixture in the wok and leave to cool. Remove and discard the lemon grass, makrut leaves and galangal. Store in an airtight container for up to 5 days. Serve with steamed rice.

PREPARATION TIME: 30 MINUTES +   COOKING TIME: 40 MINUTES

NOTE: Tempeh is an easily digestible source of protein made from soya beans. It is available from Asian grocery stores and some supermarkets and health food stores.

NOODLES AND DUMPLINGS

LION'S HEAD MEATBALLS

6 dried Chinese mushrooms
100 g (3½ oz) dried rice noodles
600 g (1 lb 5 oz) minced (ground) pork
1 egg white
4 garlic cloves, finely chopped
2 tablespoons finely grated fresh ginger
1 tablespoon cornflour (cornstarch)
1½ tablespoons Chinese rice wine
6 spring onions (scallions), thinly sliced
2 tablespoons peanut oil
1.5 litres (52 fl oz/6 cups) chicken stock diluted with 500 ml (17 floz/2 cups) water
60 ml (2 fl oz/¼ cup) light soy sauce
1 teaspoon sugar
400 g (14 oz) bok choy (pak choy), cut in half lengthways, leaves separated

SERVES 4

Put the dried mushrooms in a heatproof bowl with 250 ml (9 fl oz/1 cup) boiling water and soak for 30 minutes. Squeeze the mushrooms dry, reserving the soaking liquid. Discard the stems and chop the caps. Meanwhile, put the noodles in a heatproof bowl, cover with boiling water and soak for 4–5 minutes, or until soft. Drain and rinse.

Put the pork, egg white, garlic, ginger, cornflour, rice wine, two-thirds of the spring onion and a pinch of salt in a food processor. Using the pulse button, process until smooth and well combined. Divide the mixture into eight portions and shape into large balls using wet hands.

Heat a wok over high heat, add the peanut oil and swirl to coat the base and side. Cook the meatballs in batches for 2 minutes on each side, or until golden but not cooked through. Remove and drain on paper towel.

Clean and dry the wok, then pour the stock into the wok and bring to the boil. Add the meatballs, soy sauce, sugar and mushrooms with the soaking liquid, then cover and cook over low heat for 20–25 minutes, or until the meatballs are cooked through. Add the bok choy and noodles, cover and cook for 5 minutes, or until the noodles are heated through. Sprinkle with the remaining spring onion and serve.

PREPARATION TIME: 20 MINUTES +   COOKING TIME: 45 MINUTES

ROAST DUCK WITH RICE NOODLES

15 g (½ oz) dried Chinese mushrooms
40 g (1½ oz) wood ear fungus (see Note)
1 whole Chinese roast duck
1 tablespoon vegetable oil
2 teaspoons sesame oil
1 garlic clove, crushed
1 tablespoon grated fresh ginger
115 g (4 oz) fresh baby corn, cut in half diagonally
2 spring onions (scallions), thinly sliced
200 g (7 oz) snow peas (mangetout), cut in half diagonally
400 g (14 oz) bok choy (pak choy), cut into 2 cm (¾ inch) lengths
100 ml (3½ fl oz) oyster sauce
1 long red chilli, seeded and finely sliced
1.25 litres (44 fl oz/5 cups) chicken stock
1 tablespoon chopped coriander (cilantro) leaves
1 tablespoon torn Thai basil
400 g (14 oz) fresh rice noodle sheets, cut into 2 cm (¾ inch) strips

SERVES 4–6

Put the Chinese mushrooms in a heatproof bowl, cover with boiling water and soak for 30 minutes. Squeeze the mushrooms dry, discard the stems and finely chop the caps. Put the wood ear fungus in a heatproof bowl, cover with boiling water and soak for 20 minutes, or until soft. Drain and cut into bite-sized pieces.

Remove the meat from the duck and thinly slice. Put the bones in a large saucepan with 2.75 litres (96 fl oz/11 cups) water. Bring to the boil over high heat, then reduce the heat and simmer for 30 minutes. Remove any scum from the surface, then strain through a fine sieve.

Heat a wok over high heat, add the vegetable and sesame oils and swirl to coat the base and side. Add the garlic and ginger and fry for 30 seconds. Add the duck meat and stir-fry for 1 minute. Add the Chinese mushrooms, wood ear fungus, corn, spring onion, snow peas and bok choy and stir-fry for 2 minutes. Stir in the oyster sauce, chilli and stock and simmer for 2 minutes, or until heated through. Stir in the herbs.

Cover the noodles with boiling water and soak for 1–2 minutes, or until tender. Separate gently and drain. Divide among the bowls, then ladle the soup on top.

PREPARATION TIME: 30 MINUTES +   COOKING TIME: 45 MINUTES

NOTE: Wood ear (also called black fungus) is a cultivated wood fungus. It is mainly available dried; it needs to be reconstituted in boiling water for a few minutes until it expands to five times its dried size, before cooking.

VEGETABLE DUMPLINGS

8 dried shiitake mushrooms
1 tablespoon vegetable oil
2 teaspoons finely chopped fresh ginger
2 garlic cloves, crushed
pinch white pepper
100 g (3½ oz/1½ cups) garlic chives, chopped
100 g (3½ oz) water spinach (ong choy), cut into 1 cm (½ inch) lengths
60 ml (2 fl oz/¼ cup) chicken stock
2 tablespoons oyster sauce
1 tablespoon cornflour (cornstarch)
1 teaspoon soy sauce
1 teaspoon Chinese rice wine
45 g (1½ oz/¼ cup) tinned water chestnuts, chopped
chilli sauce, to serve

WRAPPERS
200 g (7 oz) wheat starch (see Note)
1 teaspoon cornflour (cornstarch)
185 ml (6 fl oz/¾ cup) boiling water
oil, for kneading

MAKES 24

Put the shiitake mushrooms in a heatproof bowl, cover with boiling water and soak for 20 minutes. Squeeze the mushrooms dry, discard the stems and finely chop the caps.

Heat a wok over high heat, add the oil and swirl to coat the base and side. Add the ginger, garlic, white pepper and a pinch of salt and cook for 30 seconds. Add the chives and water spinach and cook for 1 minute.

Combine the stock, oyster sauce, cornflour, soy sauce and rice wine in a separate bowl. Add to the spinach mixture along with the water chestnuts and mushrooms. Cook for 1-2 minutes, or until the mixture thickens, then remove from the heat and cool completely.

To make the wrappers, combine the wheat starch and cornflour in a bowl. Make a well in the centre and add the boiling water, a little at a time, while bringing the mixture together with your hands. When it is combined, immediately knead it using lightly oiled hands until the dough forms a shiny ball.

Keeping the dough covered with a cloth while you work, pick walnut-sized pieces from the dough and, using well-oiled hands, squash them between the palms of your hands. Roll the pieces out as thinly as possible into rounds no larger than 10 cm (4 inches) in diameter. Place 1 tablespoon of the filling in the centre of each round. Pinch the edges of the wrapper together to enclose the filling and form a tight ball.

Line a bamboo steamer with baking paper. Place the dumplings in a single layer in the steamer, leaving a gap between each one. Cover and steam each batch over a wok of simmering water for 7-8 minutes. Serve with chilli sauce.

PREPARATION TIME: 40 MINUTES +   COOKING TIME: 20 MINUTES

NOTE: Wheat starch is a very fine white powder similar to cornflour (cornstarch) in texture. It is available at Asian grocery stores.

PORK NOODLE SALAD

BROTH
250 ml (9 fl oz/1 cup) chicken stock
3 coriander (cilantro) roots
2 makrut (kaffir lime) leaves
3 cm (1¼ inch) piece fresh ginger, sliced

100 g (3½ oz) dried rice vermicelli
30 g (1 oz) wood ear fungus (see Note)
1 small red chilli, seeded and thinly sliced
2 red Asian shallots, thinly sliced
2 spring onions (scallions), thinly sliced
2 garlic cloves, crushed
250 g (9 oz) minced (ground) pork
60 ml (2 fl oz/¼ cup) lime juice
60 ml (2 fl oz/¼ cup) fish sauce
1½ tablespoons grated palm sugar (jaggery)
¼ teaspoon ground white pepper
1 large handful coriander (cilantro) leaves, chopped
oakleaf or coral lettuce, to serve
lime wedges, to garnish
chilli strips, to garnish
coriander (cilantro) leaves, extra, to garnish

SERVES 4-6

To make the broth, combine the stock, coriander roots, makrut leaves, ginger and 250 ml (9 fl oz/1 cup) water in a saucepan. Simmer for 25 minutes, or until the liquid has reduced to 185 ml (6 fl oz/¾ cup). Strain and return to the pan.

Soak the vermicelli in a saucepan of boiling water for 6-7 minutes. Drain, then cut into 3 cm (1¼ inch) lengths. Discard the woody stems from the wood ear, then thinly slice. Combine the vermicelli, wood ear, chilli, shallots, spring onion and garlic.

Return the broth to the heat and bring to a boil. Add the pork and stir, breaking up any lumps, for 1-2 minutes, or until the pork changes colour and is cooked. Drain, then add to the vermicelli mixture.

In a separate bowl, combine the lime juice, fish sauce, palm sugar and white pepper, stirring until the sugar has dissolved. Add to the pork mixture along with the coriander and mix well. Season with salt.

To assemble, tear or shred the lettuce, then arrange on a serving dish. Spoon the pork and noodle mixture on the lettuce and garnish with the lime wedges, chilli and extra coriander.

PREPARATION TIME: 20 MINUTES +   COOKING TIME: 35 MINUTES

NOTE: Wood ear (also called black fungus) is a cultivated wood fungus. It is mainly available dried; it needs to be reconstituted in boiling water for a few minutes until it expands to five times its dried size, before cooking.

STEAMED RICE NOODLE ROLLS

PORK FILLING

350 g (12 oz) Chinese barbecued pork
(char siu), chopped

3 spring onions (scallions), finely chopped

2 tablespoons chopped coriander
(cilantro) leaves

OR PRAWN FILLING

250 g (9 oz) small raw prawns (shrimp)

1 tablespoon oil

ground white pepper

3 spring onions (scallions), finely chopped

2 tablespoons chopped coriander
(cilantro) leaves

OR VEGETABLE FILLING

300 g (10½ oz) Chinese broccoli (gai larn)

1 teaspoon light soy sauce

1 teaspoon sesame oil

2 spring onions (scallions), chopped

4 fresh rice noodle rolls, at room
temperature

oyster sauce, to serve

MAKES 4

To make the pork filling, combine the pork with the spring onion and coriander.

To make the prawn filling, peel the prawns and gently pull out the dark vein from each prawn back, starting from the head end. Heat a wok over high heat, add the oil and swirl to coat the base and side. When the oil is hot, add the prawns and stir-fry for 1 minute, or until they are pink and cooked through. Season with a little salt and ground white pepper. Add the spring onion and coriander and mix well.

To make the vegetable filling, wash the Chinese broccoli well. Discard any tough looking stems and chop the rest. Put on a plate in a steamer, cover with a lid and steam over a wok of simmering water for 3 minutes, or until the stems and leaves are just tender. Combine the Chinese broccoli with the soy sauce, sesame oil and spring onion.

Carefully unroll the rice noodle rolls (don't worry if they crack or tear a little at the sides). Trim each one into a neat rectangle about 15 x 18 cm (6 x 7 inches) (you may be able to get two out of one roll if they are very large). Divide the filling among the rolls, then re-roll the noodles.

Put the rolls on a plate in a large steamer, cover and steam over a wok of simmering water for 5 minutes. Serve the rolls cut into pieces and drizzle with some oyster sauce.

PREPARATION TIME: 15 MINUTES   COOKING TIME: 10 MINUTES

CINNAMON BEEF NOODLES

1 teaspoon oil
10 spring onions (scallions), cut into 4 cm (1½ inch) lengths, lightly crushed
10 garlic cloves, thinly sliced
6 slices fresh ginger
1½ teaspoons chilli bean paste
2 cassia or cinnamon sticks (see Note)
2 star anise
125 ml (4 fl oz/½ cup) light soy sauce
1 kg (2 lb 4 oz) chuck steak, trimmed and cut into 4 cm (1½ inch) cubes
250 g (9 oz) dried rice stick noodles
250 g (9 oz) baby English spinach
3 tablespoons finely chopped spring onion (scallions)

SERVES 6

Heat a wok over medium heat, add the oil, swirl to coat the base and side, and heat until hot. Add the spring onion, garlic, ginger, chilli bean paste, cassia and star anise and stir-fry for 10 seconds, or until fragrant.

Transfer to a clay pot, casserole dish or saucepan. Add the soy sauce and 2.25 litres (79 fl oz/9 cups) water. Bring to the boil, add the beef, then return to the boil. Reduce the heat and simmer, covered, for 1½ hours, or until the beef is very tender. Skim the surface occasionally to remove any impurities and fat. Remove and discard the ginger and cassia.

Meanwhile, soak the noodles in hot water for 10 minutes, then drain and divide among six soup bowls.

Add the spinach to the beef and bring to the boil. Spoon the beef mixture over the noodles and sprinkle with the spring onion, to serve.

PREPARATION TIME: 15 MINUTES   COOKING TIME: 1 HOUR 40 MINUTES

NOTE: In China cassia bark is more often used than cinnamon to make this recipe. The bark of the cassia tree is similar to cinnamon, but the flavour is more woody.

SPINACH AND WATER CHESTNUT DUMPLINGS

DIPPING SAUCE
½ teaspoon sesame oil
½ teaspoon peanut oil
1 tablespoon soy sauce
1 tablespoon lime juice
1 small red chilli, seeded and finely chopped

FILLING
1 tablespoon peanut oil
1 teaspoon sesame oil
1 garlic clove, crushed
2.5 cm (1 inch) piece fresh ginger, grated
2 tablespoons chopped garlic chives
30 g (1 oz) water spinach (ong choy), chopped into 1 cm (½ inch) lengths
120 g (4¼ oz) tinned water chestnuts, drained, then finely chopped
1 tablespoon soy sauce

PASTRY
350 g (12 oz/2 cups) rice flour
85 g (3 oz/⅔ cup) tapioca starch
2 tablespoons arrowroot flour
1 tablespoon glutinous rice flour
tapioca flour, for dusting

MAKES 30

To make the dipping sauce, whisk all the ingredients together in a small bowl and set aside.

To make the filling, add the peanut and sesame oils to a wok over medium heat and swirl to coat the base and side. Add the garlic and ginger and cook, stirring, for 1 minute, or until fragrant but not brown. Add the chives, water spinach, water chestnuts and soy sauce and cook for 2 minutes. Remove from the wok and cool for about 5 minutes. Drain and discard any liquid.

To make the pastry, combine the rice flour, tapioca starch, arrowroot and rice flour in a large saucepan with 625 ml (21½ fl oz/2½ cups) water, stirring to remove any lumps. Stir over low heat for 10 minutes, or until thick. Cook, stirring, for a further 5 minutes, or until the liquid is opaque. Turn out onto a work surface dusted liberally with tapioca flour and cool for 10 minutes. (You will need to use the tapioca flour to continually dust the surface and your hands while kneading.) With floured hands, knead the dough for 10 minutes or until smooth and elastic. Divide into two portions, covering one half with plastic wrap.

Roll out the dough to 2 mm (⅟₁₆ inch) thick. Cut out 9 cm (3½ inch) rounds with a cutter. Place a heaped teaspoon of filling in the centre of each circle, dampen the edge with lukewarm water, fold over and pleat to seal. Place on a lightly floured board or tray and repeat with the remaining dough and filling. Do not re-roll any pastry scraps. Before steaming, lightly brush the dumplings with oil.

Line a bamboo steamer with lightly oiled baking paper. Arrange the dumplings in the steamer, leaving a gap between each one. Cover and steam each batch over a wok of simmering water for 10 minutes, or until the pastry is opaque. Repeat until all the dumplings are cooked, then serve with the dipping sauce on the side.

PREPARATION TIME: 1 HOUR 30 MINUTES +   COOKING TIME: 50 MINUTES

SCALLOP AND SNOW PEA SPROUT DUMPLINGS

½ teaspoon baking soda

250 g (9 oz) snow pea (mangetout) sprouts, cut into 1 cm (½ inch) pieces

250 g (9 oz) scallop meat, white part only

1 teaspoon finely grated fresh ginger

1½ tablespoons oyster sauce

1 teaspoon light soy sauce

1 teaspoon Chinese rice wine

½ teaspoon sesame oil

1½ teaspoons sugar

1 teaspoon cornflour (cornstarch)

1 egg white

24 gow gee wrappers

MAKES 24

Bring a saucepan of salted water to the boil, add the baking soda and the snow pea sprouts and blanch for 10 seconds. Drain and refresh under cold water. Drain thoroughly until dry.

Put the scallops in a food processor with the ginger, oyster sauce, soy sauce, rice wine, sesame oil, sugar, cornflour, egg white and ¼ teaspoon salt and blend until evenly mixed. Transfer to a bowl, cover and refrigerate for 4 hours. Add the snow pea sprouts and mix thoroughly.

Place 2 teaspoons of the filling in the centre of each gow gee wrapper, wet the edges and gather together to cover the filling, then squeeze shut, making a round bundle. Break off any surplus dough. Line a double bamboo steamer with baking paper. Place the dumplings in the steamer in a single layer, seam side down, leaving a gap between each one. Cover and steam over a wok of simmering water for 8 minutes, or until cooked through.

PREPARATION TIME: 30 MINUTES +   COOKING TIME: 10 MINUTES

CHIANG MAI NOODLES

500 g (1 lb 2 oz) hokkien (egg) noodles

1 tablespoon oil

3 red Asian shallots, chopped

6 garlic cloves, chopped

2 teaspoons finely chopped red chilli, (optional)

1–2 tablespoons red curry paste

350 g (12 oz) lean chicken or pork, thinly sliced

1 carrot, cut into thin strips

2 tablespoons fish sauce

2 teaspoons soft brown sugar

3 spring onions (scallions), thinly sliced

1 handful coriander (cilantro) leaves

SERVES 4

Cook the noodles in a wok or saucepan of rapidly boiling water for 2–3 minutes, or until they are just tender. Drain, set aside and keep warm.

Heat the oil in a wok or large frying pan until it is very hot. Add the shallots, garlic, chilli and curry paste and stir-fry for 2 minutes, or until fragrant. Add the chicken or pork and cook for 3 minutes, or until the meat changes colour. Add the carrot, fish sauce and sugar and bring to the boil.

Divide the noodles among serving bowls and add the meat and spring onion mixture evenly over the top. Scatter with coriander and serve immediately.

PREPARATION TIME: 20 MINUTES   COOKING TIME: 15 MINUTES

Scallop and snow pea sprout dumplings

SOUP DUMPLINGS

200 g (7 oz) minced (ground) pork
100 g (3½ oz) raw prawn (shrimp) meat
2 teaspoons grated fresh ginger
2 garlic cloves, crushed
1 spring onion (scallion), finely chopped
3 teaspoons Chinese rice wine
2 teaspoons soy sauce
½ teaspoon sesame oil
pinch ground white pepper
3 tablespoons beaten egg white
3 teaspoons cornflour (cornstarch)
185 ml (6 fl oz/¾ cup) chicken stock
1½ teaspoons powdered gelatine
24 won ton wrappers

DIPPING SAUCE
1 tablespoon dark soy sauce
3 teaspoons Chinese black vinegar
1 teaspoon sugar
2½ tablespoons finely shredded fresh ginger

MAKES 24

Put the pork, prawn meat, ginger, garlic, spring onion, rice wine, soy sauce, sesame oil and white pepper in a food processor and process until combined. Transfer to a small bowl and fold in the egg white and cornflour. Refrigerate for 4 hours, or overnight.

Meanwhile, pour the stock into a small saucepan over high heat, cover and bring to the boil. Remove from the heat, add the gelatine and stir until dissolved. Transfer to an 8 x 25 cm (3¼ x 10 inch) loaf (bar) tin and refrigerate for 1–2 hours, or until the jelly is set. Cut into 1.5 cm (⅝ inch) cubes.

To make the dipping sauce, combine the soy sauce, vinegar, sugar and 125 ml (4 fl oz/½ cup) water and stir until the sugar has dissolved. Add the ginger and set aside for 1 hour to allow the flavours to infuse.

Roll 3 teaspoons of filling into a ball using wet hands and make a deep indentation in the centre of the ball. Place a cube of jelly into the centre and cover completely with the filling.

Put in the centre of a won ton wrapper, lightly moisten the edges with water and bring the two diagonal corners up to join together. Repeat with the other two corners. Pinch along the seams to seal. Repeat with the remaining ingredients to make 23 more dumplings.

Line a double bamboo steamer with baking paper. Working in batches, place the dumplings in the steamer in a single layer, leaving a gap between each one. Cover and steam over a wok of simmering water for 5–6 minutes, or until cooked through. Serve with the dipping sauce on the side.

PREPARATION TIME: 45 MINUTES +   COOKING TIME: 10 MINUTES

UDON NOODLE SOUP

400 g (14 oz) dried udon noodles
1 litre (35 fl oz/4 cups) water
3 teaspoons dashi granules
2 leeks, white part only, finely sliced
200 g (7 oz) pork loin, cut into thin strips
125 ml (4 fl oz/½ cup) Japanese soy sauce
2 tablespoons mirin
4 spring onions (scallions), finely chopped
shichimi togarashi (see Note), to serve

SERVES 4

Cook the noodles in a large saucepan of rapidly boiling water for 5 minutes, or until tender. Drain and cover to keep warm.

Combine the water and dashi in a large saucepan and bring to the boil. Add the leek, reduce the heat and simmer for 5 minutes. Add the pork, soy sauce, mirin and spring onion and simmer for 2 minutes, or until the pork is cooked. Divide the noodles among four serving bowls and ladle the soup over the top. Garnish with the spring onion and sprinkle the shichimi togarashi over the top.

PREPARATION TIME: 20 MINUTES   COOKING TIME: 16 MINUTES

NOTE: Shichimi togarashi is a Japanese spice mix containing seven flavours. Ingredients can vary, but it always contains *togarashi*, a hot Japanese chilli. It is available in Asian or Japanese grocery stores.

CLASSIC STEAMED PORK AND PRAWN DUMPLINGS

300 g (10 oz) minced (ground) pork
300 g (10 oz) minced (ground) prawn (shrimp) meat
3 spring onions (scallions), thinly sliced
60 g (2¼ oz/⅓ cup) chopped tinned water chestnuts
1½ teaspoons finely chopped fresh ginger
1 tablespoon light soy sauce
1 teaspoon caster (superfine) sugar
24 won ton wrappers
soy sauce, extra, to serve
chilli sauce, to serve

MAKES 24

To make the filling, put the pork and prawn meat, spring onion, water chestnuts, ginger, soy sauce and sugar in large non-metallic bowl and combine well.

Working with one wrapper at a time, place a heaped tablespoon of the filling in the centre of the wrapper. Bring the sides up around the outside, forming pleats to firmly encase the filling — the top of the dumpling should be exposed. Pinch together to enclose the bottom of the filling, then cover with a damp cloth. Repeat with the remaining wrappers and filling to make 24 dumplings in total.

Line a large double bamboo steamer with baking paper. Place the dumplings in the steamer in a single layer, leaving a gap between each one. Cover and steam over a wok of simmering water for 5 minutes, or until cooked through. Serve the dumplings with the soy and chilli sauces, for dipping.

PREPARATION TIME: 25 MINUTES   COOKING TIME: 5 MINUTES

CHILLED SOBA NOODLES

250 g (9 oz) dried soba (buckwheat) noodles
4 cm (1½ inch) piece fresh ginger
1 carrot
4 spring onions (scallions), outside layer removed
1 sheet nori, to garnish
pickled ginger, to garnish
thinly sliced pickled daikon, to garnish

DIPPING SAUCE
3 tablespoons dashi granules
125 ml (4 fl oz/½ cup) Japanese soy sauce
80 ml (2½ fl oz/⅓ cup) mirin

SERVES 4

Put the noodles in a large saucepan of boiling water. When the water returns to the boil, pour in 250 ml (9 fl oz/1 cup) cold water. Bring the water back to the boil and cook the noodles for 2–3 minutes, or until just tender — take care not to overcook them. Drain the noodles in a colander and then cool under cold running water. Drain thoroughly and set aside.

Cut the ginger and carrot into fine matchsticks about 4 cm (1½ inches) long. Slice the spring onions very finely. Bring a small saucepan of water to the boil, add the ginger, carrot and spring onion and blanch for about 30 seconds. Drain and place in a bowl of iced water to cool. Drain again when the vegetables are cool.

To make the dipping sauce, combine 375 ml (13 fl oz/1½ cups) water, the dashi granules, soy sauce, mirin and a good pinch each of salt and pepper in a small saucepan. Bring the sauce to the boil, then cool completely. When ready to serve, pour the sauce into four small dipping bowls.

Gently toss the cooled noodles and vegetables to combine. Arrange in four individual serving bowls.

Toast the nori by holding it with tongs over low heat and moving it back and forward for about 15 seconds. Cut it into thin strips with scissors, and scatter the strips over the noodles. Place a little pickled ginger and daikon on the side of each plate. Serve the noodles with the dipping sauce. The noodles should be dipped into the sauce before being eaten.

PREPARATION TIME: 25 MINUTES   COOKING TIME: 15 MINUTES

PRAWN GOW GEES

300 g (10½ oz) raw prawns (shrimp)
100 g (3½ oz) minced (ground) pork
4 spring onions (scallions), white part only,
finely chopped
25 g (1 oz) tinned bamboo shoots,
finely chopped
1 egg white
1 teaspoon finely chopped fresh ginger
1 teaspoon sesame oil
¼ teaspoon ground white pepper
24 round gow gee wrappers

DIPPING SAUCE
60 ml (2 fl oz/¼ cup) soy sauce
1 tablespoon Chinese red vinegar
¼ teaspoon sesame oil

MAKES 24

Peel the prawns and gently pull out the dark vein from each prawn back, starting from the head end. Finely chop the prawn meat.

To make the filling, mix the chopped prawns, pork, spring onion, bamboo shoots, egg white, ginger, sesame oil, white pepper and 1 teaspoon salt in a bowl until well combined. Cover with plastic wrap and refrigerate for at least 1 hour.

Put one gow gee wrapper on a work surface and place 2 teaspoons of the filling in the centre — position the filling in an oblong shape across the wrapper, rather than a round lump. Lightly moisten the edge of the wrapper with water. Pick up the wrapper and fold the edges together to form a semi-circle. Using your thumb and index finger, create a row of pleats along the outside edge of the gow gee, pressing firmly. Twist the corners down to seal and form a crescent shape. Make sure the gow gee is completely sealed or the filling will leak out during steaming. Repeat with the remaining wrappers and filling to create 24 gow gees in total.

Line a large double bamboo steamer with baking paper. Arrange the gow gees in the steamer in a single layer, leaving a gap between each one. Cover and steam over a wok of simmering water for 8 minutes, or until cooked through.

Meanwhile, to make the dipping sauce, combine the soy sauce, red vinegar and sesame oil. Serve with the hot gow gees.

PREPARATION TIME: 40 MINUTES +   COOKING TIME: 15 MINUTES

NOODLES WITH FISH AND BLACK BEANS

270 g (9½ oz) fresh rice noodles
200 g (7 oz) Chinese broccoli (gai larn),
cut into 5 cm (2 inch) lengths
550 g (1 lb 4 oz) skinless firm white fish
fillets, cut into bite-sized pieces
2 tablespoons light soy sauce
1½ tablespoons Chinese rice wine
1 teaspoon sugar
½ teaspoon sesame oil
2 teaspoons cornflour (cornstarch)
1 tablespoon vegetable oil
5 garlic cloves, crushed
2 teaspoons finely chopped fresh ginger
2 spring onions (scallions), finely chopped
2 small red chillies, finely chopped
2 tablespoons salted black beans, rinsed
and roughly chopped (see Note)
155 ml (5 fl oz) fish stock
spring onions (scallions), sliced, extra,
to garnish

SERVES 4

Cover the noodles with boiling water and soak for 1–2 minutes, or until tender. Separate gently and drain. Keep warm.

Put the Chinese broccoli in a steamer, cover and steam over a wok of simmering water for 3–4 minutes, or until slightly wilted. Remove from the heat and keep warm.

Place the fish pieces in a bowl. Combine the soy sauce, rice wine, sugar, sesame oil and cornflour, then pour the mixture over the fish and toss to coat well.

Heat a wok over high heat until very hot, add the vegetable oil and swirl to coat the base and side. Add the garlic, ginger, spring onion, chilli and black beans and stir-fry for 1 minute. Add the fish and the marinade and cook for 2 minutes, or until the fish is almost cooked through. Remove the fish with a slotted spoon and keep warm.

Pour the fish stock into the wok and bring to the boil. Reduce the heat to low and bring to a slow simmer. Cook for 5 minutes, or until the sauce has slightly thickened. Return the fish to the wok, cover with a lid and continue to simmer gently for 2–3 minutes, or until just cooked.

To serve, divide the noodles among serving dishes, top with the Chinese broccoli and spoon the fish and black bean sauce on top. Garnish with the extra spring onion.

PREPARATION TIME: 10 MINUTES   COOKING TIME: 20 MINUTES

NOTE: Black beans are fermented and heavily salted black soy beans, and are available tinned or in packets. Rinse thoroughly before use and, once opened, store in an airtight container in the refrigerator.

RICE NOODLES WITH BEEF

500 g (1 lb 2 oz) fresh rice noodle sheets
2 tablespoons peanut oil
2 eggs, lightly beaten
500 g (1 lb 2 oz) rump steak, thinly sliced across the grain
60 ml (2 fl oz/¼ cup) kecap manis
1½ tablespoons soy sauce
1½ tablespoons fish sauce
300 g (10½ oz) Chinese broccoli (gai larn), cut into 5 cm (2 inch) lengths
¼ teaspoon ground white pepper
lemon wedges, to serve

SERVES 4–6

Cut the noodle sheets lengthways into 2 cm (¾ inch) strips. Cover with boiling water, then gently separate the strips. Set aside.

Heat a wok over medium heat, add 1 tablespoon of the oil and swirl to coat the base and side. Add the egg, swirl to coat and cook for 1–2 minutes, or until set. Remove, roll up and cut into shreds.

Reheat the wok over high heat, add the remaining oil and swirl to coat. Add the beef in batches and stir-fry for 3 minutes, or until brown. Remove the beef from the wok and set aside.

Reduce the heat to medium, add the noodles and stir-fry for 2 minutes. Combine the kecap manis, soy sauce and fish sauce. Add to the wok along with the broccoli and white pepper, then stir-fry for a further 2 minutes. Return the egg and beef to the wok and stir-fry for another 3 minutes, or until the the noodles are soft. Serve with lemon wedges.

PREPARATION TIME: 20 MINUTES   COOKING TIME: 20 MINUTES

COMBINATION DIM SIMS

6 dried Chinese mushrooms
200 g (7 oz) lean minced (ground) pork
30 g (1 oz) pork fat, finely chopped
100 g (3½ oz) raw prawn (shrimp) meat, finely chopped
2 spring onions (scallions), finely chopped
1 tablespoon finely chopped tinned bamboo shoots
1 celery stalk, finely chopped
3 teaspoons cornflour (cornstarch)
2 teaspoons soy sauce
1 teaspoon caster (superfine) sugar
30 won ton wrappers
chilli sauce or soy sauce, to serve

MAKES 30

Put the mushrooms in a small heatproof bowl, cover with boiling water and soak for 10 minutes. Squeeze the mushrooms dry, discard the stems and finely chop the caps.

Combine the mushrooms, pork, pork fat, prawn meat, spring onion, bamboo shoots and celery in a bowl. Combine the cornflour, soy sauce, and sugar in another bowl and stir to make a smooth paste. Season and then stir into the pork mixture. Cover and refrigerate for 1 hour.

Working with one won ton wrapper at a time, place 1 tablespoon of filling in the centre of each wrapper. Moisten the edges with water and gather the edges into the centre, pressing together to seal. Set aside on a lightly floured surface. Line a bamboo steamer with baking paper. Arrange the dim sims in the steamer, leaving a gap between each one. Cover and steam each batch over a wok of simmering water for 8 minutes, or until the filling is cooked. Serve with chilli sauce or soy sauce.

PREPARATION TIME: 1 HOUR +   COOKING TIME: 30 MINUTES

Rice noodles with beef

GYOZA

150 g (5½ oz) Chinese cabbage
(wong bok), finely shredded
225 g (8 oz) minced (ground) pork
2 garlic cloves, finely chopped
2 teaspoons finely chopped fresh ginger
2 spring onions (scallions), finely chopped
2 teaspoons cornflour (cornstarch)
1 tablespoon light soy sauce
2 teaspoons Chinese rice wine
2 teaspoons sesame oil
40 round Shanghai dumpling wrappers
2 tablespoons vegetable oil
125 ml (4 fl oz/½ cup) chicken stock
soy sauce or Chinese black vinegar,
to serve

MAKES 40

Put the Chinese cabbage and ½ teaspoon salt in a colander, then sit the colander in a large bowl. Toss the cabbage and then leave for 30 minutes to drain. Stir occasionally. This process will draw the liquid out of the cabbage and prevent the filling from going soggy.

Put the pork, garlic, ginger, spring onion, cornflour, soy sauce, rice wine and sesame oil in a bowl and mix with your hands.

Rinse the cabbage under cold running water. Press dry between layers of paper towel. Add to the pork mixture and combine well.

Place 1 teaspoon of the mixture in the centre of each wrapper, brushing the inside edge of the wrapper with a little water. Bring the two edges of the wrapper together to form a semi-circle. Using your thumb and index finger, create a pleat, pressing firmly and gently tapping the gyoza on a work surface to form a flat bottom. Repeat with the remaining wrappers and filling.

Heat a quarter of the oil in a wok over medium–high heat. Working in batches, cook the gyoza for 2 minutes, flat side down. Reduce the heat and add a quarter of the stock, shaking the wok gently to unstick the gyoza. Cover and steam for 4 minutes, or until the liquid has evaporated. Remove and keep warm. Repeat with the remaining oil, gyoza and stock. Serve with soy sauce or Chinese black vinegar, for dipping.

PREPARATION TIME: 50 MINUTES +   COOKING TIME: 25 MINUTES

ANTS CLIMBING TREES

1 teaspoon cornflour (cornstarch)

1½ tablespoons light soy sauce

2 tablespoons Chinese rice wine

1 teaspoon sesame oil

200 g (7 oz) minced (ground) pork

150 g (5½ oz) cellophane noodles

2 tablespoons vegetable oil

4 spring onions (scallions), finely chopped

1 garlic clove, crushed

1 tablespoon finely chopped fresh ginger

2 teaspoons chilli bean sauce

185 ml (6 fl oz/¾ cup) chicken stock

½ teaspoon sugar

2 spring onions (scallions), finely sliced, extra, to garnish

SERVES 4

Combine the cornflour, 1 tablespoon each of the soy sauce and rice wine and ½ teaspoon of the sesame oil in a large non-metallic bowl. Add the pork and use a fork or your fingers to combine the ingredients and break up any lumps. Cover with plastic wrap and marinate in the refrigerator for 10–15 minutes.

Meanwhile, put the noodles in a heatproof bowl, cover with boiling water and soak for 3–4 minutes. Rinse and drain well.

Heat a wok over high heat, add the vegetable oil and swirl to coat the base and side. Add the spring onion, garlic, ginger and chilli bean sauce and cook for 10 seconds, then add the pork and cook for 2 minutes, stirring to break up any lumps. Stir in the stock, sugar, ½ teaspoon salt and the remaining soy sauce, rice wine and sesame oil.

Add the noodles to the wok and toss to combine. Bring to the boil, then reduce the heat to low and simmer, stirring occasionally, for 7–8 minutes, or until the liquid is almost completely absorbed. Garnish with the extra spring onion and serve.

PREPARATION TIME: 20 MINUTES +   COOKING TIME: 15 MINUTES

NOTE: This Chinese dish gets its name from the pork (ants) climbing the noodles (trees).

STEAMED PORK AND WATER CHESTNUT DUMPLINGS

DOUGH

125 g (4½ oz/1 cup) plain (all-purpose) flour

60 g (2¼ oz/½ cup) tapioca flour

30 g (1 oz) lard

185 ml (6 fl oz/¾ cup) boiling water

250 g (9 oz) minced (ground) pork

50 g (1¾ oz/⅓ cup) tinned water chestnuts, chopped

2 spring onions (scallions), chopped

1 teaspoon chopped fresh ginger

2 teaspoons soy sauce

1 teaspoon rice wine

½ teaspoon sugar

½ teaspoon cornflour (cornstarch)

1 egg

¼ teaspoon sesame oil

MAKES 24

To make the dough, put the flours and lard in a food processor. Process for several seconds until combined. With the motor running, slowly add the boiling water to form a sticky, thick dough. Place the dough onto a lightly floured surface and knead for a couple of minutes. Roll into a ball, wrap in plastic wrap and set aside for 30 minutes.

To make the filling, put the pork, water chestnuts, spring onion, ginger, soy sauce, rice wine, sugar, cornflour, egg, sesame oil and ½ teaspoon salt in a food processor. Process for several seconds to evenly combine the mixture. Transfer to a bowl.

Divide the dough into four equal pieces. Roll each piece into a log about 10 cm (4 inches) long and 2 cm (¾ inch) in diameter. Cut each log into six pieces, each about 1.5 cm (⅝ inch) wide, then cover with a damp cloth.

Place each dough piece on a lightly oiled surface and flatten with the oiled flat side of a cleaver to form a very thin, small disc about 10–12 cm (4–4½ inches) in diameter.

Place 2 teaspoons of the filling into the centre of the dough wrapper and bring the edges together, pressing firmly and pulling upwards, twisting in one direction, pulling off any excess dough and making sure the dough is not too thick on top.

Line a large bamboo steamer with baking paper. Arrange the dumplings in a single layer in the steamer, leaving a gap between each one. Cover and steam each batch over a wok of simmering water for 6 minutes, or until cooked through. Serve immediately.

PREPARATION TIME: 25 MINUTES +   COOKING TIME: 10 MINUTES

PHAD THAI

250 g (9 oz) dried rice stick noodles
1 tablespoon tamarind purée
1 small red chilli, chopped
2 garlic cloves, chopped
2 spring onions (scallions), sliced
1½ tablespoons sugar
2 tablespoons fish sauce
2 tablespoons lime juice
2 tablespoons oil
2 eggs, beaten
8 large raw prawns (shrimp)
150 g (5½ oz) pork fillet, thinly sliced
100 g (3½ oz) fried tofu puffs, cut into thin strips
90 g (3¼ oz/1 cup) bean sprouts
40 g (1½ oz/¼ cup) chopped roasted peanuts
3 tablespoons coriander (cilantro) leaves
1 lime, cut into wedges

SERVES 4–6

Put the noodles in a heatproof bowl, cover with warm water and soak for 15–20 minutes, or until soft and pliable. Drain well.

Combine the tamarind purée with 1 tablespoon water. Put the chilli, garlic and spring onion in a spice grinder or mortar and pestle and grind to a smooth paste. Transfer the mixture to a bowl. Stir in the tamarind mixture along with the sugar, fish sauce and lime juice, stirring until combined.

Heat a wok until very hot, add 1 tablespoon of the oil and swirl to coat the base and side. Add the egg, swirl to coat and cook for 1–2 minutes, or until set. Remove, roll up and cut into thin slices.

Peel the prawns and gently pull out the dark vein from each prawn back, starting from the head end.

Heat the remaining oil in the wok, stir in the chilli mixture and stir-fry for 30 seconds. Add the pork and stir-fry for 2 minutes, or until tender. Add the prawns and stir-fry for a further minute, or until pink and curled.

Stir in the noodles, egg, tofu and bean sprouts and gently toss everything together until heated through. Serve immediately topped with the peanuts, coriander and lime wedges.

PREPARATION TIME: 30 MINUTES +   COOKING TIME: 10 MINUTES

CURRY MEE NOODLES

2 large dried red chillies
1 teaspoon shrimp paste
400 g (14 oz) hokkien (egg) noodles
1 onion, chopped
4 garlic cloves, chopped
4 lemon grass stems, white part only, thinly sliced
1 teaspoon grated fresh ginger
500 ml (17 fl oz/2 cups) coconut cream
25 g (1 oz/¼ cup) Malaysian curry powder
400 g (14 oz) boneless, skinless chicken thighs, thinly sliced
120 g (4¼ oz) green beans, trimmed and cut into 5 cm (2 inch) lengths
750 ml (26 fl oz/3 cups) chicken stock
10 fried tofu puffs, halved diagonally
2 tablespoons fish sauce
2 teaspoons sugar
180 g (6 oz/2 cups) bean sprouts
2 hard-boiled eggs, quartered
2 tablespoons crisp fried shallots
lime wedges, to serve

Soak the chillies in boiling water for 20 minutes. Drain, then chop. Wrap the shrimp paste in foil and put under a hot grill (broiler) for 1-2 minutes. Unwrap the shrimp paste.

Put the noodles in a bowl, cover with boiling water and soak for 1 minute to separate. Rinse under cold water, drain and set aside.

Put the onion, garlic, lemon grass, ginger, chilli and shrimp paste in a food processor or blender and process to a rough paste, adding a little water if necessary.

Put 250 ml (9 fl oz/1 cup) of the coconut cream in a wok and bring to the boil, then simmer for 10 minutes, or until the oil starts to separate from the cream. Stir in the paste and curry powder and cook for 5 minutes, or until fragrant. Add the chicken and beans and cook for 3-4 minutes, or until the chicken is almost cooked. Add the stock, tofu puffs, fish sauce, sugar and the remaining coconut cream. Simmer, covered, over low heat for 10 minutes, or until the chicken is cooked.

Divide the noodles and bean sprouts among four bowls, then ladle the curry over the top. Garnish with the egg quarters and crisp fried shallots. Serve with the lime wedges.

SERVES 4   PREPARATION TIME: 30 MINUTES +   COOKING TIME: 30 MINUTES

MANY MUSHROOM NOODLES

25 g (1 oz) dried shiitake mushrooms
375 ml (13 fl oz/1½ cups) boiling water
500 g (1 lb 2 oz) thin hokkien (egg)
noodles, separated
1 tablespoon vegetable oil
½ teaspoon sesame oil
1 tablespoon finely chopped fresh ginger
4 garlic cloves, crushed
100 g (3½ oz) fresh shiitake mushrooms,
trimmed, sliced
150 g (5½ oz) oyster mushrooms, sliced
150 g (5½ oz) shimeji mushrooms,
trimmed, pulled apart
1½ teaspoons dashi granules dissolved in
185 ml (6 fl oz/¾ cup) water
60 ml (2 fl oz/¼ cup) soy sauce
60 ml (2 fl oz/¼ cup) mirin
¼ teaspoon white pepper
25 g (1 oz) butter
2 tablespoons lemon juice
100 g (3½ oz) enoki mushrooms, trimmed,
pulled apart
1 tablespoon chopped chives

SERVES 4–6

Put the dried shiitake mushrooms in a heatproof bowl, cover with the boiling water and soak for 20 minutes, or until soft. Drain, reserving the soaking water. Squeeze the mushrooms dry, discard the stems and slice the caps.

Cover the noodles with boiling water for 1 minute, then drain and rinse. Set aside.

Heat a wok over high heat, add the oils and swirl to coat the base and side. Add the ginger, garlic, fresh shiitake, oyster and shimeji mushrooms and stir-fry for 1–2 minutes, or until the mushrooms have wilted. Remove from the wok. Set aside.

Combine the dashi, soy sauce, mirin, white pepper and 185 ml (6 fl oz/¾ cup) of the reserved liquid, add to the wok and cook for 3 minutes. Add the butter, lemon juice and 1 teaspoon salt and cook for 1 minute, or until the sauce thickens. Return the mushrooms to the wok, cook for a further 2 minutes, then stir in the enoki and sliced shiitake mushroom caps. Add the noodles and stir for 3 minutes, or until heated through. Sprinkle with the chives and serve immediately.

PREPARATION TIME: 30 MINUTES +   COOKING TIME: 15 MINUTES

SHANGHAI PORK NOODLES

½ teaspoon sesame oil

60 ml (2 fl oz/¼ cup) soy sauce

2 tablespoons oyster sauce

250 g (9 oz) pork loin fillet, cut into very thin strips

2 tablespoons dried shrimp

8 dried shiitake mushrooms

1 teaspoon sugar

250 ml (9 fl oz/1 cup) chicken stock

300 g (10½ oz) fresh Shanghai noodles

2 tablespoons peanut oil

1 garlic clove, thinly sliced

2 teaspoons grated fresh ginger

1 celery stalk, cut into matchsticks

1 leek, white part only, cut into matchsticks

150 g (5½ oz) Chinese cabbage (wong bok), shredded

50 g (1¾ oz) tinned bamboo shoots, cut into matchsticks

8 spring onions (scallions), thinly sliced

SERVES 4

Combine the sesame oil and 1 tablespoon each of the soy sauce and oyster sauce in a large non-metallic bowl. Add the pork strips and toss in the marinade. Cover and marinate in the refrigerator for 30 minutes.

Meanwhile, put the dried shrimp in a bowl, cover with boiling water and soak for 20 minutes. Drain and finely chop. At the same time, put the shiitake mushrooms in a heatproof bowl, cover with boiling water and soak for 20 minutes. Drain, squeeze the mushrooms dry, discard the stems and thinly slice the caps.

To make the stir-fry sauce, combine the sugar, stock, remaining soy and oyster sauces and 1 teaspoon salt in a small non-metallic bowl. Set aside.

Cook the noodles in a large saucepan of boiling water for 4–5 minutes, or until tender. Drain and refresh under cold water. Toss with 1 teaspoon of the peanut oil.

Heat a wok over high heat, add 1 tablespoon of the peanut oil and swirl to coat the base and side. Add the pork and stir-fry for 1–2 minutes, or until the pork is no longer pink. Transfer to a plate.

Heat the remaining peanut oil, add the garlic, ginger, celery, leek and cabbage and stir-fry for 1 minute, or until softened. Add the bamboo shoots, spring onion, shrimp and mushrooms and stir-fry for 1 minute. Add the noodles and the stir-fry sauce and toss together for 3–5 minutes, or until the noodles absorb the sauce.

Return the pork to the wok, with any juices, and toss for 1–2 minutes, or until combined and heated through. Serve immediately.

PREPARATION TIME: 25 MINUTES +   COOKING TIME: 20 MINUTES

HISS AND SIZZLE

CHICKEN WITH ALMONDS AND ASPARAGUS

2 teaspoons cornflour (cornstarch)
80 ml (2½ fl oz/⅓ cup) chicken stock
¼ teaspoon sesame oil
2 tablespoons oyster sauce
1 tablespoon soy sauce
3 garlic cloves, crushed
1 teaspoon finely chopped fresh ginger
pinch ground white pepper
2½ tablespoons peanut oil
50 g (1¾ oz/⅓ cup) blanched almonds
2 spring onions (scallions), cut into 3 cm (1¼ inch) lengths
500 g (1 lb 2 oz) boneless, skinless chicken thighs, cut into thin strips
1 small carrot, thinly sliced
155 g (5½ oz) asparagus, trimmed and cut into 3 cm (1¼ inch) lengths
60 g (2¼ oz/¼ cup) tinned bamboo shoots, sliced
steamed rice, to serve

SERVES 4–6

To make the stir-fry sauce, put the cornflour and stock in a small bowl and mix to form a paste, then stir in the sesame oil, oyster sauce, soy sauce, garlic, ginger and white pepper. Set aside until needed.

Heat a wok over high heat, add 2 teaspoons of the peanut oil and swirl to coat the base and side. Add the almonds and stir-fry for 1–2 minutes, or until golden — be careful not to burn them. Remove from the wok and drain on crumpled paper towel.

Heat another teaspoon of the peanut oil in the wok and swirl to coat. Add the spring onion and stir-fry for 30 seconds, or until wilted. Remove from the wok and set aside.

Heat 1 tablespoon of the peanut oil in the wok over high heat, add the chicken in two batches and stir-fry for 3 minutes, or until the chicken is just cooked through. Set aside with the spring onion.

Add the remaining peanut oil to the wok, then add the carrot and stir-fry for 1–2 minutes, or until just starting to brown. Toss in the asparagus and the bamboo shoots and stir-fry for a further 1 minute. Remove all the vegetables from the wok and set aside with the chicken and spring onion.

Stir the stir-fry sauce briefly, then pour into the wok, stirring until the mixture thickens. Return the chicken and vegetables to the wok and stir thoroughly for a couple of minutes until they are coated in the sauce and are heated through. Transfer to a serving dish and sprinkle with the almonds before serving. Serve with steamed rice.

PREPARATION TIME: 15 MINUTES   COOKING TIME: 15 MINUTES

LEMON GRASS BEEF

3 garlic cloves, finely chopped
1 tablespoon grated fresh ginger
4 lemon grass stems, white part only, finely chopped
2½ tablespoons vegetable oil
600 g (1 lb 5 oz) lean beef fillet, thinly sliced across the grain
1 tablespoon lime juice
1–2 tablespoons fish sauce
2 tablespoons kecap manis
1 large red onion, cut into small wedges
200 g (7 oz) green beans, sliced
steamed rice, to serve

SERVES 4

Combine the garlic, ginger, lemon grass and 2 teaspoons of the oil in a large non-metallic bowl. Add the beef, toss well to coat in the marinade, then cover with plastic wrap and refrigerate for at least 10 minutes.

To make the stir-fry sauce, combine the lime juice, fish sauce and kecap manis in a small bowl and set aside until needed.

Heat a wok over high heat, add 1 tablespoon of the oil and swirl to coat the base and side. Stir-fry the beef in batches for 2–3 minutes, or until browned. Remove from the wok and set aside.

Heat the remaining oil in the wok over high heat. Add the onion and stir-fry for 2 minutes. Add the beans and cook for a further 2 minutes, then return the beef to the wok. Pour in the stir-fry sauce and cook until heated through. Serve with steamed rice.

PREPARATION TIME: 15 MINUTES +   COOKING TIME: 25 MINUTES

STIR-FRIED LAMB AND LEEK

2 garlic cloves, crushed
2½ teaspoons dark soy sauce
2 teaspoons Chinese rice wine
2 teaspoons sesame oil
1½ teaspoons rice vinegar
1½ teaspoons cornflour (cornstarch)
1½ teaspoons sugar
350 g (12 oz) lamb loin fillets, thinly sliced across the grain
4 small leeks, white part only
60 ml (2 fl oz/¼ cup) peanut oil
1 tablespoon finely chopped fresh ginger
1 tablespoon Chinese rice wine
noodles or steamed rice, to serve

SERVES 4

Combine the garlic, soy sauce, rice wine, sesame oil, rice vinegar, cornflour, sugar and ¼ teaspoon salt in a large non-metallic bowl. Add the lamb and toss well to coat. Cover with plastic wrap and refrigerate for at least 1 hour.

Cut the leeks in half lengthways, then into 2 cm (¾ inch) lengths. Wash the leek, being careful not to break the pieces up too much. Drain well.

Heat a wok over high heat, add 1½ tablespoons of the peanut oil and swirl to coat the base and side. Add the leek and ¼ teaspoon salt and stir-fry for 1–2 minutes, or until the leek is tender but still firm. Remove the leek from the wok and clean the wok with paper towel.

Heat the remaining oil in the wok over high heat, add the ginger and cook for 30 seconds. Add the lamb and the marinade, spreading the lamb around the wok in a thin layer, and cook for 1 minute without stirring. Toss the lamb, then cook for 30 seconds. Pour in the rice wine and return the leek to the wok. Toss until warmed through, then serve immediately with noodles or rice.

PREPARATION TIME: 10 MINUTES +   COOKING TIME: 10 MINUTES

MONGOLIAN LAMB

2 garlic cloves, crushed
2 teaspoons finely grated fresh ginger
60 ml (2 fl oz/¼ cup) Chinese rice wine
60 ml (2 fl oz/¼ cup) soy sauce
2 tablespoons hoisin sauce
1 teaspoon sesame oil
1 kg (2 lb 4 oz) lamb loin fillets, thinly sliced across the grain
80 ml (2½ fl oz/⅓ cup) peanut oil
6 spring onions (scallions), cut into 3 cm (1¼ inch) lengths
2 teaspoons chilli sauce
1½ tablespoons hoisin sauce, extra
steamed rice, to serve

SERVES 4–6

Combine the garlic, ginger, rice wine, soy sauce, hoisin sauce and sesame oil in a large non-metallic bowl. Add the lamb and toss well to coat in the marinade. Cover with plastic wrap and marinate in the refrigerator overnight, tossing occasionally.

Heat a wok over high heat, add 1 tablespoon of the peanut oil and swirl to coat the base and side. Add the spring onion and stir-fry for 1 minute, or until lightly golden. Remove, reserving the oil in the wok.

Lift the lamb out of the marinade with tongs, reserving the marinade. Add the meat to the wok in four batches and stir-fry for 1–2 minutes, or until browned but not completely cooked through, adding more oil as needed. Make sure the wok is very hot before cooking each batch. Return all the meat and any juices to the wok along with the spring onion and stir-fry for 1 minute, or until the meat is cooked through.

Remove the meat and spring onion from the wok with a slotted spoon and place in a serving bowl, retaining the liquid in the wok. Add any reserved marinade to the wok along with the chilli sauce and extra hoisin sauce, then bring to the boil and cook for 3–4 minutes, or until the sauce thickens and becomes slightly syrupy. Spoon the sauce over the lamb, toss together well and serve with steamed rice.

PREPARATION TIME: 25 MINUTES +   COOKING TIME: 15 MINUTES

CHINESE BEEF AND BLACK BEAN SAUCE

2 tablespoons rinsed and drained black beans, chopped
1 tablespoon dark soy sauce
1 tablespoon Chinese rice wine
1 garlic clove, finely chopped
1 teaspoon sugar
60 ml (2 fl oz/¼ cup) peanut oil
1 onion, cut into wedges
500 g (1 lb 2 oz) lean beef fillet, thinly sliced across the grain
½ teaspoon finely chopped fresh ginger
1 teaspoon cornflour (cornstarch)
1 teaspoon sesame oil
steamed rice, to serve

SERVES 4–6

Put the beans, soy sauce, rice wine and 60 ml (2 fl oz/¼ cup) water in a small bowl and mix. In a separate bowl, crush the garlic and sugar to a paste, using a mortar and pestle.

Heat a wok over high heat, add 1 teaspoon of the peanut oil and swirl to coat the base and side. Add the onion and stir-fry for 1–2 minutes, then transfer to a bowl and set aside. Add 1 tablespoon of the peanut oil to the wok and swirl to coat the base and side, then add half the beef and stir-fry for 5–6 minutes, or until browned. Remove to the bowl with the onion. Repeat with the remaining beef.

Add the remaining peanut oil to the wok along with the garlic paste and ginger and stir-fry for 30 seconds, or until fragrant. Add the bean mixture, onion and beef. Bring to the boil, then reduce the heat and simmer, covered, for 2 minutes.

Combine the cornflour with 1 tablespoon water, pour into the wok and stir until the sauce boils and thickens. Stir in the sesame oil and serve with steamed rice.

PREPARATION TIME: 15 MINUTES   COOKING TIME: 20 MINUTES

NASI GORENG

2 eggs
80 ml (2½ fl oz/⅓ cup) oil
3 garlic cloves, finely chopped
1 onion, finely chopped
2 red chillies, seeded and very finely chopped
1 teaspoon shrimp paste
1 teaspoon coriander seeds
½ teaspoon sugar
400 g (14 oz) raw prawns (shrimp), peeled and deveined
200 g (7 oz) rump steak, thinly sliced
200 g (7 oz/1 cup) long-grain rice, cooked and cooled
2 teaspoons kecap manis
1 tablespoon soy sauce
4 spring onions (scallions), finely chopped
½ lettuce, finely shredded
1 cucumber, thinly sliced
3 tablespoons crisp fried onion

SERVES 4

Beat the eggs and ¼ teaspoon salt together until foamy. Heat a frying pan over medium heat and lightly brush with a little oil. Pour about one-quarter of the egg into the pan and cook for 1–2 minutes, or until the omelette sets. Turn the omelette over and cook the other side for about 30 seconds. Remove from the pan and repeat with the remaining egg mixture, working with one-quarter of the egg mixture at a time. Allow the omelettes to cool, then roll up, cut into strips and set aside.

Combine the garlic, onion, chilli, shrimp paste, coriander and sugar in a food processor or mortar and pestle, and process or pound to form a smooth paste.

Heat 1–2 tablespoons of the oil in a wok or large, deep frying pan. Add the paste and cook over high heat for 1 minute, or until fragrant. Add the prawns and steak and stir-fry for 2–3 minutes, or until they change colour.

Add the remaining oil and the cold rice to the wok and stir-fry, breaking up any lumps, until the rice is heated through. Add the kecap manis, soy sauce and spring onion and stir-fry for another minute.

Arrange the lettuce around the outside of a large platter. Put the rice in the centre and garnish with the omelette strips, cucumber slices and fried onion. Serve immediately.

PREPARATION TIME: 35 MINUTES   COOKING TIME: 30 MINUTES

SATAY LAMB

60 ml (2 fl oz/¼ cup) peanut oil
750 g (1 lb 10 oz) lamb loin fillets, thinly sliced across the grain
2 teaspoons ground cumin
1 teaspoon ground turmeric
1 red capsicum (pepper), seeded, membrane removed and sliced
60 ml (2 fl oz/¼ cup) sweet chilli sauce
60 g (2¼ oz/¼ cup) crunchy peanut butter
250 ml (9 fl oz/1 cup) coconut milk
2 teaspoons soft brown sugar
1–2 tablespoons lemon juice, to taste
4 tablespoons chopped coriander (cilantro) leaves
40 g (1½ oz/¼ cup) toasted unsalted peanuts, chopped, to serve
steamed rice, to serve

SERVES 4

Heat a wok over high heat, add 1 tablespoon of the peanut oil and swirl to coat the base and side. Add half the lamb and stir-fry for 3 minutes, or until browned. Remove from the wok. Repeat with another tablespoon of oil and the remaining lamb.

Reheat the wok, add the remaining oil, cumin, turmeric and capsicum and stir-fry for 2 minutes, or until the capsicum is tender.

Return the lamb to the wok. Stir in the sweet chilli sauce, peanut butter, coconut milk and sugar. Bring to the boil, then reduce the heat and simmer for 5 minutes, or until the meat is tender and the sauce has thickened slightly. Remove from the heat and add the lemon juice. Stir in the coriander and sprinkle with peanuts. Serve with steamed rice.

PREPARATION TIME: 10 MINUTES   COOKING TIME: 15 MINUTES

YANGZHOU FRIED RICE

125 g (4½ oz) cooked prawns (shrimp)
150 g (5½ oz/1 cup) fresh or frozen peas
1 tablespoon oil
3 spring onions (scallions), finely chopped
1 tablespoon finely chopped ginger
2 eggs, lightly beaten
550 g (1 lb 4 oz/3 cups) cold, cooked long-grain rice
1½ tablespoons chicken stock
1 tablespoon Chinese rice wine
2 teaspoons light soy sauce
½ teaspoon sesame oil

SERVES 6

Peel the prawns and gently pull out the dark vein from each prawn back, starting from the head end.

Cook the peas in a saucepan of simmering water for 3–4 minutes for fresh, or 1 minute if using frozen.

Heat a wok over high heat, add the oil and swirl to coat the base and side. When the oil is hot, add the spring onion and ginger and stir-fry for 1 minute. Reduce the heat, add the egg and lightly scramble. Add the prawns and peas and toss lightly to heat through, then add the rice before the egg is set too hard. Increase the heat and stir to separate the rice grains and break the egg into small bits. Add the stock, rice wine, soy sauce, sesame oil, ½ teaspoon salt and ¼ teaspoon freshly ground black pepper and toss lightly, before serving.

PREPARATION TIME: 20 MINUTES   COOKING TIME: 10 MINUTES

KUNG PAO CHICKEN

1 egg white
2 teaspoons cornflour (cornstarch)
½ teaspoon sesame oil
2 teaspoons Chinese rice wine
1½ tablespoons soy sauce
600 g (1 lb 5 oz) boneless, skinless chicken thighs, cut into small cubes
60 ml (2 fl oz/¼ cup) chicken stock
2 teaspoons Chinese black vinegar
1 teaspoon soft brown sugar
2 tablespoons vegetable oil
3 long dried red chillies, cut in half lengthways
3 garlic cloves, finely chopped
2 teaspoons finely grated fresh ginger
2 spring onions (scallions), thinly sliced
50 g (1¾ oz/⅓ cup) unsalted raw peanuts, roughly crushed

SERVES 4

Lightly whisk together the egg white, cornflour, sesame oil, rice wine and 2 teaspoons of the soy sauce in a large non-metallic bowl. Add the chicken and toss to coat in the marinade. Cover with plastic wrap and marinate in the refrigerator for 30 minutes.

To make the stir-fry sauce, combine the stock, vinegar, sugar and the remaining soy sauce in a small bowl.

Heat a wok over high heat, add 1 tablespoon of the vegetable oil and swirl to coat the base and side. Stir-fry the chicken in batches for about 3 minutes, or until browned. Remove from the wok.

Heat the remaining oil in the wok, then add the chilli and cook for 15 seconds, or until it starts to change colour. Add the garlic, ginger, spring onion and peanuts and stir-fry for 1 minute. Return the chicken to the wok along with the stir-fry sauce and stir-fry for 3 minutes, or until heated through and the sauce has thickened slightly. Serve immediately.

PREPARATION TIME: 15 MINUTES +   COOKING TIME: 15 MINUTES

NOTE: This dish is said to have been created for an important court official called Kung Pao (or Gong Bao), who was stationed in the Sichuan province of China. It is characterized by the flavours of the long, dried red chillies, popular in Sichuan cuisine, and the crunchiness of peanuts. It can also be made with meat or prawns (shrimp).

MA PO TOFU

3 teaspoons cornflour (cornstarch)
1 teaspoon oyster sauce
1 garlic clove, finely chopped
1 tablespoon soy sauce
250 g (9 oz) minced (ground) pork
1 tablespoon vegetable oil
3 teaspoons chilli bean paste
3 teaspoons preserved bean curd
750 g (1 lb 10 oz) firm tofu, drained, cubed
2 spring onions (scallions), sliced
3 teaspoons oyster sauce, extra
1½ teaspoons sugar

SERVES 4

Combine the cornflour, oyster sauce, garlic and 2 teaspoons of the soy sauce in a large bowl. Add the pork, then cover and leave to marinate for 10 minutes.

Heat a wok over high heat, add the oil and swirl to coat the base and side. Add the pork and stir-fry for 5 minutes, or until browned. Add the chilli bean paste and bean curd and cook for 2 minutes, or until fragrant. Add the remaining soy sauce, tofu, spring onion, extra oyster sauce and sugar and stir for 3–5 minutes, or until heated through.

PREPARATION TIME: 15 MINUTES +   COOKING TIME: 15 MINUTES

CHILLI PLUM BEEF

2 tablespoons vegetable oil
600 g (1 lb 5 oz) lean beef fillet, thinly sliced across the grain
1 large red onion, cut into wedges
1 red capsicum (pepper), seeded, membrane removed and finely sliced
1½ tablespoons chilli garlic sauce
125 ml (4 fl oz/½ cup) plum sauce
1 tablespoon light soy sauce
2 teaspoons rice vinegar
pinch finely ground white pepper
4 spring onions (scallions), sliced
steamed rice or noodles, to serve

SERVES 4

Heat a wok over high heat, add 1 tablespoon of the oil and swirl to coat the base and side. Stir-fry the beef in two batches for 2–3 minutes, or until browned and just cooked. Remove from the wok and set aside.

Heat the remaining oil in the wok, add the onion and stir-fry for 1 minute, then add the capsicum and stir-fry for 2–3 minutes, or until just tender. Add the chilli garlic sauce and stir for 1 minute, then return the meat to the wok and add the plum sauce, soy sauce, vinegar, white pepper and most of the spring onion.

Toss everything together for 1 minute, or until the meat is heated through. Sprinkle with the remaining spring onion and serve with steamed rice or noodles.

PREPARATION TIME: 15 MINUTES   COOKING TIME: 15 MINUTES

MEE GROB

4 dried Chinese mushrooms
8 raw prawns (shrimp)
oil, for deep-frying
100 g (3½ oz) dried rice vermicelli
100 g (3½ oz) fried tofu puffs, cut into thin strips
4 garlic cloves, crushed
1 onion, chopped
1 boneless, skinless chicken breast (about 200 g/7 oz), thinly sliced
8 green beans, sliced diagonally
6 spring onions (scallions), thinly sliced
30 g (1 oz) bean sprouts
coriander (cilantro) leaves, to garnish

SAUCE
1 tablespoon light soy sauce
60 ml (2 fl oz/¼ cup) white vinegar
60 ml (2 fl oz/¼ cup) fish sauce
1 tablespoon sweet chilli sauce
110 g (3¾ oz/½ cup) sugar

SERVES 4–6

Put the mushrooms in a heatproof bowl, cover with boiling water and soak for 20 minutes. Squeeze the mushrooms dry, discard the stems and thinly slice the caps.

Peel the prawns and gently pull out the dark vein from each prawn back, starting from the head end.

Fill a wok or heavy-based saucepan one-third full of oil and heat to 180°C (350°F), or until a cube of bread dropped into the oil browns in 15 seconds. Cook the vermicelli in batches for 5 seconds, or until puffed and crispy. Drain on paper towel.

Add the tofu to the wok in batches and deep-fry for 1 minute, or until crisp. Drain on paper towel. Cool the oil slightly and carefully remove all but 2 tablespoons of the oil.

Reheat the wok over high heat until very hot. Add the garlic and onion and stir-fry for 1 minute. Add the mushrooms, chicken, green beans and half the spring onion and stir-fry for 2 minutes, or until the chicken has almost cooked through. Add the prawns and stir-fry for a further 2 minutes, or until the prawns just turn pink.

To make the sauce, combine the soy sauce, white vinegar, fish sauce, sweet chilli sauce and sugar, stirring to dissolve the sugar. Add to the wok and stir-fry for 2 minutes, or until the sauce is syrupy and the meat and prawns are tender. Remove the wok from the heat and stir in the vermicelli, tofu and bean sprouts. Garnish with the coriander and the remaining spring onion.

PREPARATION TIME: 30 MINUTES +   COOKING TIME: 15 MINUTES

CHINESE BARBECUED PORK WITH CHINESE BROCCOLI

60 ml (2 fl oz/¼ cup) chicken or vegetable stock

60 ml (2 fl oz/¼ cup) oyster sauce

1 tablespoon kecap manis

1 kg (2 lb 4 oz) Chinese broccoli (gai larn), cut into 5 cm (2 inch) lengths

1 tablespoon peanut oil

2 cm (¾ inch) piece fresh ginger, cut into thin matchsticks

2 garlic cloves, crushed

500 g (1 lb 2 oz) Chinese barbecued pork, thinly sliced

steamed rice or noodles, to serve

SERVES 4

To make the stir-fry sauce, combine the stock, oyster sauce and kecap manis in a small bowl. Set aside until needed.

Put the Chinese broccoli in a steamer over a saucepan or wok of simmering water and cook for 5 minutes, or until just tender but still crisp.

Heat a wok over high heat, add the oil and swirl to coat the base and side. Add the ginger and garlic and stir-fry for 30 seconds, or until fragrant. Add the Chinese broccoli and pork and toss to coat. Pour in the stir-fry sauce and toss together until heated through. Serve with steamed rice or noodles.

PREPARATION TIME: 10 MINUTES   COOKING TIME: 10 MINUTES

CHILLI BEEF

60 ml (2 fl oz/¼ cup) kecap manis

2½ teaspoons sambal oelek

2 garlic cloves, crushed

½ teaspoon ground coriander

1 tablespoon grated palm sugar (jaggery)

1 teaspoon sesame oil

400 g (14 oz) lean beef fillet, thinly sliced across the grain

1 tablespoon peanut oil

2 tablespoons chopped toasted peanuts, to serve

3 tablespoons chopped coriander (cilantro) leaves, to garnish

steamed rice, to serve

SERVES 4

Combine the kecap manis, sambal oelek, garlic, ground coriander, palm sugar, sesame oil and 2 tablespoons water in a large bowl. Add the beef and toss well to coat in the marinade. Cover with plastic wrap and marinate in the refrigerator for 20 minutes.

Heat a wok over high heat, add the peanut oil and swirl to coat the base and side. Add the meat and marinade and stir-fry, in batches, for 2–3 minutes, or until browned and cooked.

Arrange the beef on a serving platter and sprinkle with the chopped peanuts and coriander. Serve with steamed rice.

PREPARATION TIME: 10 MINUTES +   COOKING TIME: 10 MINUTES

Chinese barbecued pork with Chinese broccoli

SPRING ONION LAMB

1 tablespoon Chinese rice wine
60 ml (2 fl oz/¼ cup) soy sauce
½ teaspoon white pepper
600 g (1 lb 5 oz) lean lamb loin fillets,
thinly sliced across the grain
1 tablespoon Chinese black vinegar
1 teaspoon sesame oil
2 tablespoons vegetable oil
750 g (1 lb 10 oz) choy sum, cut into 10 cm
(4 inch) lengths
3 garlic cloves, crushed
6 spring onions (scallions), cut into 10 cm
(4 inch) lengths

SERVES 4

Combine the rice wine, 1 tablespoon soy sauce, white pepper and ½ teaspoon salt in a large non-metallic bowl. Add the lamb and toss well to coat in the marinade. Cover with plastic wrap and leave to marinate in the refrigerator for at least 10 minutes.

To make the stir-fry sauce, combine the black vinegar, sesame oil and 1 tablespoon soy sauce in a small non-metallic bowl. Set aside until needed.

Heat a wok over high heat, add 2 teaspoons of the vegetable oil and swirl to coat the base and side. Add the choy sum, stir-fry briefly, then add a third of the crushed garlic and the remaining soy sauce. Cook for 3 minutes, or until cooked, but still crisp. Remove from the wok and keep warm.

Wipe the wok clean with paper towel, then reheat the wok over high heat. Add 1 tablespoon of the vegetable oil and swirl to coat the base and side. Add the lamb in two batches and stir-fry over high heat for 1–2 minutes, or until nicely browned. Remove from the wok.

Add a little more oil to the wok if necessary, then add the spring onion and remaining garlic and stir-fry for 1–2 minutes. Pour the stir-fry sauce into the wok and stir for 1 minute, or until combined. Return the lamb to the wok and continue to stir-fry for another minute, or until combined and heated through. Serve immediately with the choy sum.

PREPARATION TIME: 10 MINUTES +   COOKING TIME: 10 MINUTES

STIR-FRIED MUSHROOMS

1 tablespoon oil
2.5 cm (1 inch) piece galangal, thinly sliced
2 garlic cloves, chopped
2 red chillies, thinly sliced
200 g (7 oz) button mushrooms, halved
100 g (3½ oz) oyster mushrooms, halved
1 tablespoon fish sauce (optional)
1 teaspoon soy sauce
2 handfuls basil, chopped
steamed rice, to serve

SERVES 4 AS A SIDE

Heat the oil in a wok and swirl to coat the base and side. Add the galangal, garlic and chilli and stir-fry for 2 minutes. Add the button mushrooms and stir-fry for a further 2 minutes, then add the oyster mushrooms and stir-fry for 30 seconds, tossing constantly until the mushrooms begin to soften. Add the fish sauce, soy sauce and basil and toss well to combine. Serve immediately with a main course and steamed rice.

PREPARATION TIME: 10–15 MINUTES   COOKING TIME: 5 MINUTES

NOTE: Other varieties of mushroom may be used in this recipe.

PORK, PUMPKIN AND CASHEW STIR-FRY

2–3 tablespoons vegetable oil
80 g (2¾ oz/½ cup) cashew nuts
750 g (1 lb 10 oz) pork loin fillet, thinly sliced across the grain
500 g (1 lb 2 oz) pumpkin (winter squash), cut into cubes
1 tablespoon grated fresh ginger
80 ml (2½ fl oz/⅓ cup) chicken stock
60 ml (2 fl oz/¼ cup) dry sherry
1½ tablespoons soy sauce
½ teaspoon cornflour (cornstarch)
500 g (1 lb 2 oz) baby bok choy (pak choy), chopped
2 tablespoons coriander (cilantro) leaves
steamed rice, to serve

SERVES 4

Heat a wok over high heat, add 1 tablespoon of the oil and swirl to coat the base and side. Add the cashews and stir-fry for 1–2 minutes, or until browned. Drain and set the cashews aside.

Reheat the wok, add a little extra oil and swirl to coat the base and side. Stir-fry the pork in batches for 5 minutes, or until lightly browned, then remove from the wok and set aside. Add 1 tablespoon of the oil and stir-fry the pumpkin and ginger for 3 minutes, or until the pumpkin is lightly browned. Add the stock, sherry and soy sauce and simmer for 3 minutes, or until the pumpkin is tender.

Blend the cornflour with 1 teaspoon water, add to the wok and stir until the mixture boils and thickens. Return the cashews and pork to the wok and add the bok choy and coriander. Stir until the bok choy has just wilted. Serve with steamed rice.

PREPARATION TIME: 20 MINUTES   COOKING TIME: 20 MINUTES

Stir-fried mushrooms

CHICKEN CHOW MEIN

250 g (9 oz) fresh thin egg noodles
2 teaspoons sesame oil
125 ml (4 fl oz/½ cup) peanut oil
1 tablespoon Chinese rice wine
1½ tablespoons light soy sauce
3 teaspoons cornflour (cornstarch)
400 g (13 oz) boneless, skinless chicken breasts, cut into thin strips
1 garlic clove, crushed
1 tablespoon finely chopped fresh ginger
100 g (3½ oz) sugar snap peas, trimmed
250 g (9 oz) Chinese cabbage (wong bok), finely shredded
4 spring onions (scallions), cut into 2 cm (¾ inch) lengths
100 ml (3½ fl oz) chicken stock
1½ tablespoons oyster sauce
100 g (3½ oz) bean sprouts
1 small red chilli, seeded and very thinly sliced, to garnish (optional)

SERVES 4

Cook the noodles in a saucepan of boiling water for 1 minute, or until tender. Drain well. Add the sesame oil and 1 tablespoon of the peanut oil and toss well. Place on a baking tray and spread out in a thin layer. Leave in a dry place for at least 1 hour.

Meanwhile, combine the rice wine, 1 tablespoon soy sauce and 1 teaspoon cornflour in a large non-metallic bowl. Add the chicken and toss well to coat in the marinade. Cover with plastic wrap and marinate for 10 minutes.

Heat 1 tablespoon of the peanut oil in a small non-stick frying pan over high heat. Add one-quarter of the noodles, shaping them into a pancake. Reduce the heat to medium and cook for 4 minutes on each side, or until crisp and golden. Drain on crumpled paper towel and keep warm. Repeat with 3 tablespoons of the oil and the remaining noodles to make four noodle cakes in total.

Heat a wok over high heat, add the remaining peanut oil and swirl to coat the base and side. Stir-fry the garlic and ginger for 30 seconds, then add the chicken and stir-fry for 3-4 minutes, or until golden and tender. Add the sugar snap peas, Chinese cabbage and spring onion and stir-fry for 2 minutes, or until the cabbage has wilted. Stir in the stock, oyster sauce and bean sprouts and bring to the boil.

Combine the remaining cornflour with 1-2 teaspoons cold water. Stir the cornflour mixture into the wok along with the remaining soy sauce and cook for 1-2 minutes, or until the sauce thickens.

To assemble, place a noodle cake on each serving plate and then spoon the chicken and vegetable mixture on top. Serve immediately, garnished with chilli, if desired.

PREPARATION TIME: 15 MINUTES +   COOKING TIME: 40 MINUTES

JAPANESE PORK AND CABBAGE STIR-FRY

¼ teaspoon dashi granules
1½ tablespoons vegetable oil
500 g (1 lb 2 oz) pork loin fillet, very thinly sliced across the grain
4 spring onions (scallions), cut into 3 cm (1¼ inch) lengths
135 g (4¾ oz/3 cups) shredded Chinese cabbage (wong bok)
60 ml (2 fl oz/¼ cup) soy sauce
2 teaspoons mirin
3 teaspoons finely grated fresh ginger
2 garlic cloves, crushed
1–2 teaspoons sugar
black sesame seeds or thinly sliced spring onion (scallion), to garnish (optional)
steamed rice, to serve

SERVES 4

Dissolve the dashi in 125 ml (4 fl oz/½ cup) hot water.

Heat a wok over high heat, add 1 tablespoon of the oil and swirl to coat the base and side. Stir-fry the pork in three batches for 1 minute at a time, or until it just changes colour, then remove from the wok and set aside.

Add the remaining oil to the wok and swirl to coat, then add the spring onion and Chinese cabbage and stir-fry for 1 minute, or until softened slightly, then set aside with the pork.

Combine the dashi broth, soy sauce, mirin, ginger, garlic and sugar in a bowl. Add to the wok, bring to the boil and cook for 1 minute. Return the pork and vegetables to the wok and stir-fry for 2–3 minutes, or until combined and the pork is just cooked through but still tender.

Serve immediately with rice. If desired, garnish with black sesame seeds or thinly sliced spring onion.

PREPARATION TIME: 15 MINUTES   COOKING TIME: 10 MINUTES

TANDOORI CHICKEN WITH CARDAMOM RICE

250 g (9 oz/1 cup) Greek-style yoghurt
60 g (2¼ oz/¼ cup) tandoori paste
(see Note)
2 tablespoons lemon juice
1 kg (2 lb 4 oz) boneless, skinless chicken
breasts, cut into 4 cm (1½ inch) cubes
1 tablespoon oil
1 onion, finely diced
300 g (10½ oz/1½ cups) long-grain rice
2 cardamom pods, bruised
750 ml (26 fl oz/3 cups) hot chicken stock
400 g (14 oz) baby English spinach leaves
Greek-style yoghurt, extra, to serve

SERVES 4

Soak eight bamboo skewers in water for 30 minutes to prevent them burning during cooking.

Meanwhile, combine the yoghurt, tandoori paste and lemon juice in a non-metallic dish. Add the chicken and coat well, then cover with plastic wrap and marinate for at least 10 minutes.

Heat the oil in a saucepan, add the onion and cook for 3 minutes, then add the rice and cardamom pods. Cook, stirring often, for 3–5 minutes, or until the rice is slightly opaque. Add the hot stock and bring to the boil. Reduce the heat to low, then cover and cook the rice, without removing the lid, for 15 minutes.

Meanwhile, wash the spinach and put it in a large saucepan with just the water clinging to the leaves. Cook, covered, over medium heat for 1–2 minutes, or until the spinach has wilted. Set aside and keep warm.

Preheat a barbecue plate or grill (broiler) to very hot. Thread the chicken cubes onto the soaked bamboo skewers, leaving the bottom quarter of the skewers empty. Cook the skewers on each side for 4–5 minutes, or until the chicken is cooked through.

Uncover the rice, fluff up with a fork and serve with the spinach, chicken and a dollop of extra yoghurt.

PREPARATION TIME: 15 MINUTES +   COOKING TIME: 45 MINUTES   ·

NOTE: Tandoori paste is usually made up of a mixture of cumin, coriander, cinnamon, cloves, chilli, ginger, garlic, turmeric, mace, salt, colouring and yoghurt, though recipes do vary. There are many commercial varieties of paste available in jars from Indian grocery stores and large supermarkets.

SWEET CHILLI PRAWNS

80 ml (2½ fl oz/⅓ cup) chilli garlic sauce
2 tablespoons tomato sauce (ketchup)
2 tablespoons Chinese rice wine
1 tablespoon Chinese black vinegar
1 tablespoon soy sauce
1 tablespoon soft brown sugar
1 teaspoon cornflour (cornstarch)
1 kg (2 lb 4 oz) raw prawns (shrimp)
2 tablespoons peanut oil
3 cm (1¼ inch) piece fresh ginger,
finely sliced
2 garlic cloves, finely chopped
5 spring onions (scallions), cut into 3 cm
(1¼ inch) lengths
finely chopped spring onion (scallion),
to garnish
steamed rice, to serve

SERVES 4

To make the stir-fry sauce, combine the chilli garlic sauce, tomato sauce, rice wine, black vinegar, soy sauce and sugar in a small bowl. Dissolve the cornflour in 125 ml (4 fl oz/½ cup) water and stir into the sauce. Set aside.

Peel the prawns and gently pull out the dark vein from each prawn back, starting from the head end.

Heat a wok over high heat, add the oil and swirl to coat the base and side, then add the ginger, garlic and spring onion and stir-fry for 1 minute. Add the prawns and cook for 2 minutes, or until the prawns are pink and starting to curl. Remove from the wok.

Pour the stir-fry sauce into the wok and cook, stirring, for 1–2 minutes, or until it thickens slightly. Return the prawns to the wok for a further 2 minutes, or until heated and cooked through. Garnish with the chopped spring onion. Serve with steamed rice.

PREPARATION TIME: 20 MINUTES   COOKING TIME: 10 MINUTES

STIR-FRIED FISH WITH GINGER

1 tablespoon peanut oil
1 small onion, thinly sliced
3 teaspoons ground coriander
600 g (1 lb 5 oz) boneless white fish fillets,
cut into bite-sized strips
1 tablespoon finely shredded fresh ginger
1 teaspoon finely chopped and seeded
green chilli
2 tablespoons lime juice
2 tablespoons coriander (cilantro) leaves
steamed rice, to serve

SERVES 4

Heat a wok over high heat, add the oil and swirl to coat the base and side. Add the onion and stir-fry for 4 minutes, or until soft and golden. Add the ground coriander and cook for 1–2 minutes, or until fragrant. Add the fish, ginger and chilli and stir-fry for 5–7 minutes, or until the fish is cooked through, taking care that the fish doesn't break up. Stir in the lime juice and season to taste. Garnish with the coriander leaves and serve with steamed rice.

PREPARATION TIME: 20 MINUTES   COOKING TIME: 15 MINUTES

Sweet chilli prawns

CLAMS IN CHILLI PASTE

CHILLI PASTE
2 tablespoons oil
2 spring onions (scallions), sliced
2 garlic cloves, sliced
85 g (3 oz/¼ cup) dried shrimp
6 small fresh red chillies, seeded
2 teaspoons grated palm sugar (jaggery)
2 teaspoons fish sauce
2 teaspoons tamarind purée

1 kg (2 lb 4 oz) fresh clams (vongole)
3 garlic cloves, thinly sliced
3 small red chillies, seeded and sliced
lengthways
1 tablespoon light soy sauce
250 ml (9 fl oz/1 cup) fish or chicken stock
1 handful Thai basil
steamed rice, to serve

SERVES 4   PREPARATION TIME: 15 MINUTES   COOKING TIME: 12–15 MINUTES

To make the chilli paste, heat the oil in a wok over medium heat and fry the spring onion, garlic, dried shrimp and chilli for about 3 minutes, or until golden brown. Remove from the wok with a slotted spoon. Reserve the oil in the wok.

Place the shrimp mixture and sugar in a mortar and pestle or small food processor and pound or process until well blended. Add the fish sauce, tamarind purée and a pinch of salt and continue to blend to obtain a finely textured paste.

Soak the clams in cold water for 30 minutes. Discard any broken clams or open ones that don't close when tapped on the bench.

Heat the reserved oil in the wok. Add the garlic, chilli, soy sauce and chilli paste. Mix well, then add the stock and bring just to the boil. Add the clams and cook over medium–high heat for 2–3 minutes. Discard any unopened clams. Stir in the basil and serve immediately with steamed rice.

NOTE: Dried shrimp are available from Asian food stores. They are delicious in stir-fries and salads. Store in an airtight container.

VIETNAMESE FRIED RICE

60 ml (2 fl oz/¼ cup) fish sauce
2 tablespoons soy sauce
2 teaspoons sugar
3 eggs
125 ml (4 fl oz/½ cup) oil
1 large onion, finely chopped
6 spring onions (scallions), chopped
4 garlic cloves, finely chopped
5 cm (2 inch) piece fresh ginger, grated
2 small red chillies, seeded and finely chopped
250 g (9 oz) pork loin fillet, finely chopped
125 g (4½ oz) Chinese sausage (lap cheong), thinly sliced
100 g (3½ oz) green beans, chopped
100 g (3½ oz) carrots, chopped
½ large red capsicum (pepper), seeded, membrane removed and chopped
470 g (1 lb 1 oz/2½ cups) cold, cooked jasmine rice

SERVES 4

Combine the fish sauce, soy sauce and sugar in a bowl, stirring until the sugar dissolves. Set aside until needed.

Whisk the eggs and ¼ teaspoon salt together. Heat 1 tablespoon of the oil in a wok and swirl the oil to coat the base and side. Pour in the egg and cook over medium heat, stirring regularly for 2–3 minutes, or until just cooked. Remove from the wok.

Heat another tablespoon of oil in the wok and stir-fry the onion, spring onion, garlic, ginger and chilli for 7 minutes, or until the onion is soft, then remove from the wok. Add a little more oil and stir-fry the pork and sausage for 3–4 minutes, then remove and set aside.

Add the rest of the oil and stir-fry the beans, carrot and capsicum for 1 minute, then add the rice and cook for 2 minutes. Return everything except the egg to the wok, add the fish sauce mixture and toss. Add the egg, toss lightly to combine, and serve.

PREPARATION TIME: 30 MINUTES   COOKING TIME: 35 MINUTES

TOFU AND VEGETABLES

125 g (4½ oz) dried rice vermicelli
185 ml (6 fl oz/¾ cup) oil
1 tablespoon soy sauce
1 tablespoon sherry
1 tablespoon oyster sauce
125 ml (4 fl oz/½ cup) vegetable stock
2 teaspoons cornflour (cornstarch)
1 tablespoon oil, extra
1 garlic clove, crushed
1 teaspoon grated fresh ginger
375 g (13 oz) firm tofu, cut into small cubes
2 carrots, cut into matchsticks
250 g (9 oz) snow peas (mangetout), trimmed
4 spring onions (scallions), thinly sliced
425 g (15 oz) tinned straw mushrooms, drained

SERVES 4–6

Break the vermicelli into short lengths. Heat half the oil in a wok over medium heat. Cook the vermicelli in batches until crisp, adding more oil when necessary. Drain on paper towel.

Combine the soy sauce, sherry, oyster sauce and stock in a small bowl. Blend the cornflour with 2 teaspoons water in another small bowl.

Heat the wok, add the extra oil and cook the garlic and ginger over high heat for 1 minute. Add the tofu and stir-fry for 3 minutes. Remove the tofu from the wok and set aside.

Add the carrot and snow peas to the wok and stir-fry for 1 minute. Add the soy sauce mixture, cover and cook for a further 3 minutes, or until the vegetables are just cooked. Return the tofu to the wok. Add the spring onion, mushrooms and cornflour mixture. Stir until the sauce has thickened, then remove from the heat. Serve with the crisp vermicelli.

PREPARATION TIME: 25–30 MINUTES   COOKING TIME: 20 MINUTES

GLAZED HOISIN CHICKEN STIR-FRY

½ teaspoon sesame oil

1 egg white

1 tablespoon cornflour (cornstarch)

700 g (1 lb 9 oz) boneless, skinless chicken thighs, cut into small cubes

2 tablespoons peanut oil

2 garlic cloves, chopped

1 tablespoon finely shredded fresh ginger

1 tablespoon brown bean sauce

1 tablespoon hoisin sauce

1 tablespoon Chinese rice wine

1 teaspoon light soy sauce

4 spring onions (scallions), finely sliced

steamed rice, to serve

SERVES 4

Combine the sesame oil, egg white and cornflour in a large non-metallic bowl. Add the chicken, toss to coat in the marinade, then cover with plastic wrap and marinate in the refrigerator for at least 15 minutes.

Heat a wok over high heat, add the peanut oil and swirl to coat the base and side. Add the chicken in three batches and stir-fry for 4 minutes at a time, or until cooked through. Remove the chicken from the wok and set aside.

Reheat the wok over high heat, add a little extra oil if necessary, then add the garlic and ginger and stir-fry for 1 minute. Return the chicken to the wok and add the bean sauce and hoisin sauce and cook, stirring, for 1 minute. Add the rice wine, soy sauce and spring onion and cook for 1 minute, or until the sauce is thick and glossy and coats the chicken. Serve with steamed rice.

PREPARATION TIME: 15 MINUTES +   COOKING TIME: 15 MINUTES

GARLIC AND GINGER PRAWNS

1 kg (2 lb 4 oz) large raw prawns (shrimp)
2 tablespoons oil
3–4 garlic cloves, finely chopped
5 cm (2 inch) piece fresh ginger, cut into thin matchsticks
2–3 small red chillies, seeded and finely chopped
6 coriander (cilantro) roots, finely chopped
8 spring onions (scallions), cut diagonally into short lengths
½ red capsicum (pepper), thinly sliced
2 tablespoons lemon juice
125 ml (4 fl oz/½ cup) white wine
2 teaspoons grated palm sugar (jaggery)
2 teaspoons fish sauce, or to taste
1 tablespoon coriander (cilantro) leaves, to garnish

SERVES 4

Peel the prawns, leaving the tails intact. Gently cut a slit down the back of each prawn and remove the dark vein from each. Press each prawn out flat.

Heat a wok until very hot, add the oil and swirl to coat the base and side. Stir-fry half of the prawns, garlic, ginger, chilli and coriander root for 1–2 minutes over high heat, or until the prawns have just turned pink, then remove from the wok and set aside. Repeat with the remaining prawns, garlic, ginger, chilli and coriander root. Remove and set aside.

Add the spring onion and capsicum to the wok and cook over high heat for 2–3 minutes. Combine the lemon juice, wine and palm sugar, then add to the wok. Boil until the liquid has reduced by two-thirds.

Return the prawns to the wok and sprinkle with the fish sauce to taste. Toss until the prawns are heated through. Remove from the heat and serve sprinkled with coriander.

PREPARATION TIME: 25 MINUTES   COOKING TIME: 10 MINUTES

SHAKING BEEF

1½ tablespoons fish sauce
1½ tablespoons light soy sauce
1½ teaspoons caster (superfine) sugar
6 garlic cloves, crushed
3 spring onions (scallions), white part only, finely chopped
60 ml (2 fl oz/¼ cup) vegetable oil
750 g (1 lb 10 oz) lean beef fillet, cut into 2 cm (¾ inch) cubes
2 teaspoons rice vinegar
2 teaspoons lime juice
1 teaspoon light soy sauce, extra
100 g (3½ oz) lettuce leaves, washed, trimmed and dried, to serve
steamed rice, to serve

SERVES 4

Combine the fish sauce, soy sauce, sugar, garlic, spring onion, 1 teaspoon of the oil, ¾ teaspoon freshly ground black pepper and ½ teaspoon salt in a large non-metallic bowl. Add the beef, cover with plastic wrap and marinate in the fridge for at least 1 hour, or overnight.

To make the dressing, combine the rice vinegar, lime juice, extra soy sauce, 3 teaspoons of the oil and 2 teaspoons water in a small non-metallic bowl.

Place the lettuce leaves on a serving plate then pour on the dressing.

Heat a wok over high heat, add 1 tablespoon of the oil and swirl to coat the base and side. Add half the beef in one layer, allowing it to sit without stirring for 1 minute, so that a brown crust forms on the bottom. Stir-fry the beef briefly, or use the handle to shake the wok vigorously, tossing the beef around in the heat, for 3–4 minutes for medium–rare, or until cooked to your liking. Remove the beef from the wok then repeat with the remaining oil and beef.

Arrange the beef over the lettuce leaves and serve immediately with steamed rice.

PREPARATION TIME: 10 MINUTES +   COOKING TIME: 10 MINUTES

NOTE: The name of this dish derives from the French term 'sauté', from which the technique of shaking the meat has been borrowed.

INDONESIAN SAMBAL SQUID

1 kg (2 lb 4 oz) cleaned squid hoods
1 tablespoon white vinegar
1 tablespoon tamarind pulp
80 ml (2½ fl oz/⅓ cup) boiling water
4 red Asian shallots, finely chopped
8 small red chillies, half of them seeded, chopped
6 garlic cloves
1 lemon grass stem, white part only, chopped
2 teaspoons grated fresh ginger
½ teaspoon shrimp paste
2½ tablespoons peanut oil
½ teaspoon ground cumin
1½ tablespoons soft brown sugar
steamed rice, to serve

SERVES 6

Cut each squid hood in half lengthways and open out flat, with the inside uppermost. Score a shallow diamond pattern all over the squid hoods, taking care not to cut all the way through. Cut the hoods into 5 cm (2 inch) squares. Put the pieces in a bowl with the vinegar and 1 litre (35 fl oz/4 cups) water and soak for 10 minutes, then rinse and drain the squid and set aside.

Put the tamarind in a bowl and pour in the boiling water. Allow to steep for 5 minutes, breaking up the pulp as it softens. Strain into a bowl and discard the solids.

Put the shallots, chilli, garlic, lemon grass, ginger, shrimp paste and 1 teaspoon of the oil in a small food processor or mortar and pestle and blend or pound until a smooth paste is formed. Stir in the cumin.

Heat a non-stick wok over high heat, add 1 tablespoon of the oil and swirl to coat the base and side. Add the paste and cook for 5 minutes, or until it is fragrant, glossy and the liquid has evaporated. Remove from the wok.

Reheat the wok to very hot, add the remaining oil and swirl to coat. Add the squid pieces in small batches and stir-fry for 1–2 minutes, or until cooked through. Remove from the wok.

Reduce the heat to medium, then add the paste, strained tamarind water and sugar. Stir-fry for 2 minutes, or until the sauce ingredients are well combined. Return the squid to the wok and stir-fry for 1 minute, or until the squid is well coated with the sauce and heated through. Serve with steamed rice.

PREPARATION TIME: 20 MINUTES +   COOKING TIME: 15 MINUTES

NOTE: Use a non-stick or stainless steel wok to cook this recipe because the tamarind purée will react with the metal in a regular wok and will taint the dish.

THAI WATER SPINACH
IN FLAMES

4 garlic cloves, crushed

2 green chillies, thinly sliced

1 tablespoon black bean sauce

2 tablespoons fish sauce

2 teaspoons sugar

2 tablespoons vegetable oil

500 g (1 lb 2 oz) water spinach (ong choy),
cut into 3 cm (1¼ inch) lengths

SERVES 4

Combine the garlic, chilli, black bean sauce, fish sauce and sugar in a
small bowl.

Heat a wok over high heat, add the oil and swirl to coat the base and
side. Add the spinach and stir-fry for 1 minute, or until wilted slightly.
Add the sauce and stir-fry for 30 seconds, or until the spinach leaves
are well coated. Serve immediately.

PREPARATION TIME: 10 MINUTES   COOKING TIME: 2 MINUTES

EGGPLANT WITH CHILLI
BEAN PASTE

125 ml (4 fl oz/½ cup) vegetable stock

60 ml (2 fl oz/¼ cup) Chinese rice wine

2 tablespoons rice vinegar

1 tablespoon tomato paste
(concentrated purée)

2 teaspoons soft brown sugar

2 tablespoons soy sauce

60 ml (2 fl oz/¼ cup) peanut oil

800 g (1 lb 12 oz) eggplant (aubergine), cut
into 2 cm (¾ inch) cubes

4 spring onions (scallions), chopped

3 garlic cloves, crushed

1 tablespoon finely chopped fresh ginger

1 tablespoon chilli bean paste

1 teaspoon cornflour (cornstarch)

SERVES 4–6

Combine the stock, rice wine, rice vinegar, tomato paste, sugar and soy
sauce in a bowl.

Heat a wok over high heat, add half the oil and swirl to coat the base
and side. Stir-fry the eggplant in batches for 3 minutes at a time, or until
brown. Remove from the wok.

Heat the remaining oil in the wok. Stir-fry the spring onion, garlic, ginger
and bean paste for 30 seconds. Pour in the sauce and stir-fry for about
1 minute. Mix the cornflour with 1 tablespoon water, add to the wok and
bring to the boil. Return the eggplant to the wok and stir-fry for a further
2–3 minutes, or until heated through. Serve immediately.

PREPARATION TIME: 20 MINUTES   COOKING TIME: 15 MINUTES

Thai water spinach in flames

SPICY DRY-FRIED SHREDDED BEEF

1 tablespoon light soy sauce

½ teaspoon sesame oil

1 tablespoon Chinese rice wine

400 g (14 oz) lean beef fillet, thinly sliced across the grain, then shredded

2–3 tablespoons peanut oil

2 garlic cloves, finely chopped

1 teaspoon grated fresh ginger

3 spring onions (scallions), finely chopped

SAUCE

1½ tablespoons brown bean sauce

1 tablespoon chilli bean paste

½ teaspoon caster (superfine) sugar

½ teaspoon chilli oil

¼ teaspoon sea salt

SERVES 4

Combine the soy sauce, sesame oil, 2 teaspoons of the rice wine and ½ teaspoon salt in a large non-metallic bowl. Add the beef, cover with plastic wrap and marinate in the refrigerator for at least 2 hours.

To make the sauce, combine all the ingredients in a non-metallic bowl.

Heat a wok over high heat, add 1 tablespoon of the peanut oil and swirl to coat the base and side. Add the beef in two batches, using your hands to break up any clumps as you drop the beef into the wok. Stir-fry each batch for 1 minute, or until the beef is browned. Remove, place on crumpled paper towel and drain off any liquid from the meat.

Clean and dry the wok, then heat over high heat, add the remaining oil and swirl to coat. Add the garlic and ginger and stir-fry for 30 seconds, or until fragrant. Return the beef to the wok and cook for 2 minutes, or until it is very dry. Add the remaining 2 teaspoons of rice wine and stir-fry for 30 seconds, or until all the wine is absorbed. Add the bean sauce mixture and stir well until the beef is well coated. Remove from the heat, stir in the spring onion and serve.

PREPARATION TIME: 15 MINUTES +   COOKING TIME: 10 MINUTES

FIVE-SPICE PORK STIR-FRY

375 g (13 oz) fresh thin egg noodles

1 tablespoon sesame oil

3 teaspoons grated fresh ginger

1½ teaspoons Chinese five-spice

2 teaspoons rice flour

500 g (1 lb 2 oz) pork loin fillet, thinly
sliced across the grain

2 tablespoons vegetable oil

2 garlic cloves, crushed

1 red capsicum (pepper), thinly sliced

300 g (10½ oz) bok choy (pak choy) or
Chinese cabbage (wong bok), chopped

6 spring onions (scallions), sliced

2 tablespoons Chinese rice wine

2 tablespoons hoisin sauce

1 tablespoon soy sauce

SERVES 4

Cook the noodles in a saucepan of boiling water for 1 minute. Drain, rinse and return to the saucepan. Stir in half of the sesame oil. Set aside.

Place the ginger, five-spice and rice flour in a bowl, season, then mix well. Add the pork and toss to coat.

Heat a wok over high heat, add half of the vegetable oil and swirl to coat the base and side. Add the pork in batches and stir-fry for 5 minutes at a time, or until tender. Remove from the wok and set aside. Add the remaining vegetable oil, garlic, capsicum, bok choy and spring onion and stir-fry for 3 minutes, or until softened.

Return the pork to the wok and stir in the rice wine, hoisin sauce, soy sauce and the remaining sesame oil and simmer for 2 minutes. Add the noodles and reheat gently before serving.

PREPARATION TIME: 20 MINUTES   COOKING TIME: 20 MINUTES

GENERAL TSO'S CHICKEN

2 tablespoons Chinese rice wine
1 tablespoon cornflour (cornstarch)
80 ml (2½ fl oz/⅓ cup) dark soy sauce
3 teaspoons sesame oil
900 g (2 lb) boneless, skinless chicken thighs, cut into 3 cm (1¼ inch) cubes
2 pieces dried citrus peel
125 ml (4 fl oz/½ cup) peanut oil
1½–2 teaspoons chilli flakes
2 tablespoons finely chopped fresh ginger
60 g (2¼ oz/1 cup) thinly sliced spring onions (scallions), plus extra, to garnish
2 teaspoons sugar
steamed rice, to serve

SERVES 4–6

Combine the rice wine, cornflour, 2 tablespoons of the soy sauce and 2 teaspoons of the sesame oil in a large non-metallic bowl. Add the chicken, toss to coat in the marinade, then cover and marinate in the refrigerator for 1 hour.

Meanwhile, soak the dried citrus peel in warm water for 20 minutes. Remove from the water and finely chop — you will need 1½ teaspoons chopped peel.

Heat the peanut oil in a wok over high heat. Using a slotted spoon, drain the chicken from the marinade, then add to the wok in batches and stir-fry for 2 minutes at a time, or until browned and just cooked through. Remove from the oil with a slotted spoon and leave to drain in a colander or sieve.

Drain all the oil except 1 tablespoon from the wok. Reheat the wok over high heat, then add the chilli flakes and ginger. Stir-fry for 10 seconds, then return the chicken to the wok. Add the spring onion, sugar, chopped citrus peel, remaining soy sauce and sesame oil and ½ teaspoon salt and stir-fry for a further 2–3 minutes, or until well combined and warmed through. Garnish with the extra spring onion and serve with steamed rice.

PREPARATION TIME: 15 MINUTES +   COOKING TIME: 10 MINUTES

NOTE: This dish is named after a 19th-century Chinese general from Yunnan province.

BRAISED VEGETABLES WITH CASHEWS

1 tablespoon peanut oil
2 garlic cloves, crushed
2 teaspoons grated fresh ginger
300 g (10½ oz) choy sum, cut into 10 cm (4 inch) lengths
150 g (5½ oz) baby corn, sliced in half diagonally
185 ml (6 fl oz/¾ cup) chicken or vegetable stock
200 g (7 oz) sliced tinned bamboo shoots
150 g (5½ oz) oyster mushrooms, halved
2 teaspoons cornflour (cornstarch)
2 tablespoons oyster sauce
2 teaspoons sesame oil
90 g (3¼ oz/1 cup) bean sprouts, tailed
steamed rice, to serve
75 g (2½ oz) unsalted cashew nuts, toasted, to serve

SERVES 4

Heat a wok over medium heat, add the peanut oil and swirl to coat the base and side. Add the garlic and ginger and stir-fry for 1 minute. Increase the heat to high, add the choy sum and baby corn and stir-fry for another minute.

Add the stock and continue to cook for 3–4 minutes, or until the choy sum stems are just tender. Add the bamboo shoots and mushrooms and cook for 1 minute.

Combine the cornflour and 1 tablespoon water in a small bowl and mix into a paste. Stir the cornflour mixture and oyster sauce into the vegetables and cook for 1–2 minutes, or until the sauce is slightly thickened. Stir in the sesame oil and bean sprouts and serve immediately on a bed of steamed rice sprinkled with the toasted cashews.

PREPARATION TIME: 15 MINUTES   COOKING TIME: 10 MINUTES

CHICKEN STIR-FRY WITH SNOW PEA SPROUTS

2 tablespoons vegetable oil
1 onion, thinly sliced
3 makrut (kaffir lime) leaves, shredded
3 boneless, skinless chicken breasts, cut into 2 cm (¾ inch) cubes
1 red capsicum (pepper), sliced
60 ml (2 fl oz/¼ cup) lime juice
100 ml (3½ fl oz) soy sauce
100 g (3½ oz) snow pea (mangetout) sprouts
2 tablespoons chopped coriander (cilantro) leaves

SERVES 4

Heat a wok over medium heat, add the oil and swirl to coat the base and side. Add the onion and makrut leaves and stir-fry for 3–5 minutes, or until the onion begins to soften. Add the chicken and cook for 4 minutes, then add the capsicum and stir-fry for 2–3 minutes.

Stir in the lime juice and soy sauce and cook for 1–2 minutes, or until the sauce reduces slightly. Toss in the sprouts and coriander and cook until the sprouts have wilted slightly. Serve immediately with steamed rice, if desired.

PREPARATION TIME: 15 MINUTES   COOKING TIME: 15 MINUTES

Braised vegetables with cashews

YAKISOBA

4 dried shiitake mushrooms
600 g (1 lb 5 oz) hokkien (egg) noodles
3 teaspoons finely chopped fresh ginger
2 large garlic cloves, finely chopped
300 g (10½ oz) lean beef fillet, thinly
sliced across the grain
6 streaky bacon slices, cut into 3 cm
(1¼ inch) pieces
2 tablespoons peanut oil
½ teaspoon sesame oil
6 thin spring onions (scallions), cut into
3 cm (1¼ inch) lengths
1 carrot, thinly sliced
1 small green capsicum (pepper), thinly
sliced
220 g (7¾ oz) Chinese cabbage (wong
bok), shredded
pickled ginger, to serve (optional)
shredded nori, to serve (optional)

SAUCE
60 ml (2 fl oz/¼ cup) Japanese soy sauce
2 tablespoons worcestershire sauce
1½ tablespoons Japanese rice vinegar
1 tablespoon sake
1 tablespoon mirin
1 tablespoon tomato sauce (ketchup)
1 tablespoon oyster sauce
2 teaspoons soft brown sugar

SERVES 4

Put the shiitake mushrooms in a heatproof bowl, cover with boiling water and soak for 20 minutes, or until soft. Squeeze the mushrooms dry, reserving 2 tablespoons of the soaking liquid, discard the stems and thinly slice the caps.

Put the noodles in a heatproof bowl, cover with boiling water and soak for 1 minute. Drain and separate the noodles.

Combine half the ginger and half the garlic in a small bowl, add the beef and toss to coat. Set aside.

To make the sauce, combine all the ingredients in a bowl along with the reserved mushroom liquid and the remaining ginger and garlic.

Heat a wok over medium–high heat, add the bacon and cook for about 2–3 minutes, or until softened and just starting to brown. Transfer to a large bowl. Combine the peanut and sesame oils. Increase the heat to high, add a little of the oil mixture to the wok and stir-fry the beef very quickly for 1 minute, or until it just changes colour all over. Set aside with the bacon.

Heat a little more of the oil mixture in the wok, add the spring onion, carrot and capsicum and stir-fry for 1 minute. Add the Chinese cabbage and mushrooms and cook for another 30 seconds, or until the vegetables are just cooked but still tender, then add to the bowl with the bacon.

Heat the remaining oil in the wok, add the noodles and stir-fry for 1 minute, then return the bacon, beef and vegetables to the wok, pour on the sauce and stir-fry for 2–3 minutes, or until heated through (the sauce shouldn't be too runny; it should be almost completely absorbed but not dry). Divide the noodles among four deep bowls and top with pickled ginger and shredded nori, if desired.

PREPARATION TIME: 30 MINUTES +   COOKING TIME: 10 MINUTES

STIR-FRIED BABY OCTOPUS

500 g (1 lb 2 oz) baby octopus
3 tablespoons chopped coriander
(cilantro) leaves
2 garlic cloves, finely chopped
2 red chillies, seeded and chopped
2 teaspoons grated fresh ginger
2 lemon grass stems, white part only,
chopped
3 tablespoons vegetable oil
2 tablespoons lime juice
550 g (1 lb 4 oz) bok choy (pak choy),
leaves separated
400 g (14 oz) choy sum, leaves separated
2 garlic cloves, crushed, extra
1 teaspoon grated fresh ginger, extra

SERVES 4

To prepare baby octopus, remove the head, cut off the eyes and remove the gut by slitting the head open. Grasp the body firmly and push the beak out with your index finger. Clean the octopus thoroughly under cold running water and pat dry with paper towel. Cut each head into two or three pieces.

Combine the coriander, garlic, chilli, ginger, lemon grass, 1 tablespoon vegetable oil and lime juice in a large non-metallic bowl. Add the octopus, cover with plastic wrap and refrigerate for at least 2 hours, or overnight.

Heat a wok over high heat, add 1 tablespoon of the oil and swirl to coat the base and side. Add the bok choy and choy sum along with 1 tablespoon water and stir-fry for 3 minutes, or until wilted. Remove from the wok and arrange on a serving plate.

Reheat the wok, add 1 tablespoon of the oil and stir-fry the extra garlic and ginger for 30 seconds, or until fragrant. Add the octopus and stir-fry over high heat for 7–8 minutes, or until cooked through. Serve on the bed of wilted greens.

PREPARATION TIME: 30 MINUTES +   COOKING TIME: 10 MINUTES

CANTONESE LEMON CHICKEN

500 g (1 lb 2 oz) boneless, skinless
chicken breasts
1 egg yolk, lightly beaten
2 teaspoons soy sauce
2 teaspoons dry sherry
3 teaspoons cornflour (cornstarch)
60 g (2¼ oz/½ cup) cornflour
(cornstarch), extra
2½ tablespoons plain (all-purpose) flour
oil, for deep-frying
4 spring onions (scallions), thinly sliced

LEMON SAUCE
80 ml (2½ fl oz/⅓ cup) lemon juice
2 tablespoons sugar
1 tablespoon dry sherry
2 teaspoons cornflour (cornstarch)

SERVES 4

Cut the chicken into long strips, about 1 cm (½ inch) wide, and then set aside. Combine the egg, 1 tablespoon water, soy sauce, sherry and cornflour in a small bowl and mix until smooth. Pour the egg mixture over the chicken, mixing well, and set aside for 10 minutes.

Sift the extra cornflour and plain flour together onto a plate. Roll each piece of chicken in the flour, coating each piece evenly, and shake off the excess. Place the chicken in a single layer on a plate.

Fill a wok one-third full of oil and heat to 180°C (350°F), or until a cube of bread dropped into the oil browns in 15 seconds. Carefully lower the chicken pieces into the oil, in batches, and cook for 2 minutes, or until golden brown. Remove the chicken with a slotted spoon and drain on paper towel. Repeat with the remaining chicken. Set aside while preparing the sauce. Reserve the oil in the wok.

To make the lemon sauce, combine 2 tablespoons water, the lemon juice, sugar and sherry in a small saucepan. Bring to the boil over medium heat, stirring until the sugar dissolves. Stir the cornflour into 1 tablespoon water and mix to a smooth paste, then add to the lemon juice mixture, stirring constantly until the sauce boils and thickens. Set aside.

Just before serving, reheat the oil in the wok to very hot, add all the chicken pieces and deep-fry for 2 minutes, or until very crisp and a rich golden brown. Remove the chicken with a slotted spoon and drain well on paper towel. Pile the chicken onto a serving plate, drizzle over the sauce, sprinkle with spring onion and serve immediately.

PREPARATION TIME: 15 MINUTES   COOKING TIME: 25 MINUTES

NOTE: The first deep-frying of the chicken pieces can be done several hours in advance.

BEEF WITH MANDARIN

2 teaspoons soy sauce
2 teaspoons dry sherry
1 teaspoon chopped fresh ginger
1 teaspoon sesame oil
350 g (12 oz) rib eye steak, thinly sliced
1 tablespoon peanut oil
¼ teaspoon ground white pepper
2 teaspoons finely chopped dried mandarin or tangerine peel
2 teaspoons soy sauce, extra
1½ teaspoons caster (superfine) sugar
1½ teaspoons cornflour (cornstarch)
80 ml (2½ fl oz/⅓ cup) beef stock
steamed rice, to serve

SERVES 4

Combine the soy sauce, sherry, ginger and sesame oil in a bowl. Add the beef and stir to coat in the marinade. Set aside for 15 minutes.

Heat the peanut oil in a wok, swirling gently to coat the base and side. Add the beef and stir-fry over high heat for 2 minutes, or until the meat changes colour. Add the white pepper, peel, extra soy sauce and sugar and stir-fry briefly.

Dissolve the cornflour in a little of the stock, then add to the wok. Add the remaining stock and stir until the sauce boils and thickens. Serve with steamed rice.

PREPARATION TIME: 15 MINUTES +   COOKING TIME: 5 MINUTES

STIR-FRIED CHICKEN WITH LEMON GRASS, GINGER AND CHILLI

2 tablespoons oil
2 brown onions, roughly chopped
4 garlic cloves, finely chopped
5 cm (2 inch) piece ginger, grated
3 lemon grass stems, white part only, thinly sliced
2 teaspoons chopped green chilli
500 g (1 lb 2 oz) boneless, skinless chicken thighs, thinly sliced
2 teaspoons sugar
1 tablespoon fish sauce
finely chopped coriander (cilantro) leaves and Vietnamese mint, to garnish

SERVES 4

Heat the oil in a heavy-based frying pan or wok over medium heat. Add the onion, garlic, ginger, lemon grass and chilli and stir-fry for 3–5 minutes, or until the mixture is lightly golden. Take care not to burn the mixture or it will become bitter.

Increase heat to high and when the pan is very hot, add the chicken and toss well. Sprinkle the sugar over the chicken and cook for about 5 minutes, tossing regularly until the chicken is just cooked. Add the fish sauce, cook for a further 2 minutes, then serve immediately, garnished with the coriander and Vietnamese mint.

PREPARATION TIME: 30 MINUTES   COOKING TIME: 20 MINUTES

SEARED SCALLOPS WITH CHILLI BEAN PASTE

500 g (1 lb 2 oz) hokkien (egg) noodles
60 ml (2 fl oz/¼ cup) peanut oil
20 scallops, roe removed
1 large onion, cut into thin wedges
3 garlic cloves, crushed
1 tablespoon grated fresh ginger
1 tablespoon chilli bean paste
150 g (5½ oz) choy sum, cut into 5 cm
(2 inch) lengths
60 ml (2 fl oz/¼ cup) chicken stock
2 tablespoons light soy sauce
2 tablespoons kecap manis
1 handful coriander (cilantro) leaves
90 g (3¼ oz/1 cup) bean sprouts, washed
1 large red chilli, seeded and thinly sliced
1 teaspoon sesame oil
1 tablespoon Chinese rice wine

SERVES 4

Put the noodles in a heatproof bowl, cover with boiling water and soak for 1 minute to separate. Drain, rinse, then drain again. Set aside.

Heat a wok over high heat, add 2 tablespoons peanut oil and swirl to coat the base and side. Add the scallops in batches and sear for 20 seconds on each side, or until sealed. Remove from the wok and set aside.

Add the remaining peanut oil to the wok and swirl to coat. Stir-fry the onion for 1–2 minutes, or until softened. Add the garlic and ginger and cook for 30 seconds. Stir in the chilli bean paste and cook for 1 minute, or until fragrant. Add the choy sum, noodles, stock, soy sauce and kecap manis. Stir-fry for 4 minutes, or until the choy sum has wilted and the noodles have absorbed most of the liquid. Return the scallops to the wok, add the coriander, bean sprouts, chilli, sesame oil and rice wine, tossing gently until combined. Serve immediately.

PREPARATION TIME: 20 MINUTES   COOKING TIME: 15 MINUTES

CUCUMBER AND WHITE FISH STIR-FRY

60 g (2¼ oz/½ cup) plain (all-purpose) flour
60 g (2¼ oz/½ cup) cornflour (cornstarch)
½ teaspoon Chinese five-spice
750 g (1 lb 10 oz) boneless, firm white fish fillets, cut into 3 cm (1¼ inch) cubes
2 egg whites, lightly beaten
oil, for deep-frying
1 tablespoon vegetable oil
1 onion, cut into wedges
1 telegraph (long) cucumber, halved, seeded and sliced diagonally
1 teaspoon cornflour (cornstarch), extra
¾ teaspoon sesame oil
1 tablespoon soy sauce
80 ml (2½ fl oz/⅓ cup) rice vinegar
1½ tablespoons soft brown sugar
3 teaspoons fish sauce

SERVES 4

Combine the plain flour, cornflour and five-spice in a shallow bowl and season. Dip the fish in the beaten egg white, drain off any excess, then toss gently in the flour mixture, shaking off any excess.

Fill a large saucepan one-third full of oil and heat to 180°C (350°F), or until a cube of bread dropped into the oil browns in 15 seconds. Cook the fish, in batches, for 6 minutes, or until golden brown. Drain on crumpled paper towel.

Heat a wok over high heat, add the vegetable oil and swirl to coat the base and side. Add the onion and stir-fry for 1 minute, then add the cucumber and stir-fry for 30 seconds.

Blend the extra cornflour with 2 tablespoons water and add to the wok along with the sesame oil, soy sauce, rice vinegar, sugar and fish sauce. Stir-fry for 3 minutes, or until the mixture boils and thickens. Add the fish and toss thoroughly to coat in the sauce and heat through. Serve hot.

PREPARATION TIME: 20 MINUTES   COOKING TIME: 20 MINUTES

STIR-FRIED TOFU AND BOK CHOY

600 g (1 lb 5 oz) firm tofu, cut into cubes
1 tablespoon finely chopped fresh ginger
2 tablespoons soy sauce
2 tablespoons peanut oil
1 red onion, thinly sliced
4 garlic cloves, crushed
500 g (1 lb 2 oz) baby bok choy (pak choy), sliced lengthways
2 teaspoons sesame oil
2 tablespoons kecap manis
60 ml (2 fl oz/¼ cup) sweet chilli sauce
1 tablespoon toasted sesame seeds

SERVES 4

Put the tofu and ginger in a bowl. Pour in the soy sauce and leave for 10 minutes. Drain.

Heat a wok over high heat, add half the peanut oil and swirl to coat the base and side. Add the onion and stir-fry for 3 minutes, or until soft. Add the tofu and garlic and stir-fry for 3 minutes. Remove from the wok.

Reheat the wok to very hot, add the remaining oil and the bok choy and stir-fry for 2 minutes, or until wilted. Return the tofu mixture to the wok and toss until heated through. Stir in the sesame oil, kecap manis and chilli sauce. Scatter with the sesame seeds and serve.

PREPARATION TIME: 20 MINUTES +   COOKING TIME: 10 MINUTES

Cucumber and white fish stir-fry

SIMMER AND SPICE

THAI GREEN CHICKEN CURRY

CURRY PASTE

1 tablespoon shrimp paste

1 teaspoon coriander seeds, toasted

1/2 teaspoon cumin seeds, toasted

1/4 teaspoon white peppercorns

5 coriander (cilantro) roots

3 tablespoons chopped fresh galangal

10 long green chillies, chopped

1 lemon grass stem, white part only, chopped

6 red Asian shallots

3 garlic cloves

1 teaspoon grated lime zest

2 tablespoons peanut oil

250 ml (9 fl oz/1 cup) coconut cream

500 g (1 lb 2 oz) boneless, skinless chicken thighs, thinly sliced

125 g (4 1/2 oz) snake (yard-long) beans, sliced

500 ml (17 fl oz/2 cups) coconut milk

150 g (5 1/2 oz) broccoli, cut into small florets

1 tablespoon grated palm sugar

2-3 tablespoons fish sauce

5 tablespoons coriander (cilantro) leaves, plus extra, to garnish

steamed rice, to serve

SERVES 4

To make the curry paste, preheat the grill (broiler) to high, wrap the shrimp paste in foil, and put under the hot grill for 5 minutes. Cool, remove the foil then put the shrimp paste in a food processor.

Put the coriander seeds, cumin seeds and peppercorns in a mortar and pestle and grind to a fine powder. Transfer to the food processor with 1/4 teaspoon salt and the remaining paste ingredients. Blend until smooth.

Put the coconut cream in a wok over high heat, bring to the boil then simmer for 10 minutes, or until the oil starts to separate from the cream. Reduce the heat to medium. Stir in half the curry paste and cook for 2-3 minutes, or until fragrant. Add the chicken and cook for 3-4 minutes. Stir in the beans, coconut milk and broccoli. Bring to the boil then reduce the heat and simmer for 4-5 minutes, or until cooked. Stir in the sugar, fish sauce and coriander leaves. Garnish with the extra coriander and serve with steamed rice.

PREPARATION TIME: 15 MINUTES   COOKING TIME: 30 MINUTES

NOTE: Store the remaining curry paste in an airtight container in the refrigerator for up to 2 weeks.

HOISIN BEEF STEW

1½ tablespoons peanut oil

1 kg (2 lb 2 oz) chuck beef steak, cut into 3 cm (1¼ inch) cubes

1 tablespoon finely chopped fresh ginger

1 tablespoon finely chopped garlic

1 litre (35 fl oz/4 cups) beef stock

80 ml (2½ fl oz/⅓ cup) Chinese rice wine

80 ml (2½ fl oz/⅓ cup) hoisin sauce

5 cm (2 inch) piece cassia bark

1 piece dried tangerine peel

2 star anise

1 teaspoon sichuan peppercorns, lightly crushed

2 teaspoons brown sugar

300 g (10½ oz) daikon, cut into 3 cm (1¼ inch) chunks

3 spring onions (scallions), cut into 3 cm (1¼ inch) lengths, plus extra, to garnish

50 g (1¾ oz) tinned bamboo shoots, sliced

a few drops sesame oil (optional)

steamed rice, to serve

SERVES 6

Heat a wok until very hot, add the peanut oil and swirl to coat the base and side. Stir-fry the beef in batches for 1–2 minutes, or until browned all over. Remove from the wok and set aside.

Add the ginger and garlic to the wok and stir-fry for a few seconds. Add the stock, rice wine, hoisin sauce, cassia bark, tangerine peel, star anise, sichuan peppercorns, sugar, daikon and 875 ml (30 fl oz/3½ cups) water then return the beef to the wok. Bring to the boil, skimming any scum that forms on the surface, then reduce to a simmer and cook, stirring occasionally for 1½ hours, or until the beef is tender and the sauce has thickened slightly. Add the spring onion and the bamboo shoots 5 minutes before the end of the cooking time. Stir in a few drops of sesame oil and garnish with extra spring onion, if desired. Serve with steamed rice.

PREPARATION TIME: 15 MINUTES   COOKING TIME: 1 HOUR 45 MINUTES

NOTE: You can remove the star anise, cassia bark and tangerine peel before serving or leave them in the serving dish for presentation.

LAMB KORMA

2 kg (4 lb 8 oz) leg of lamb, boned
1 onion, chopped
2 teaspoons grated fresh ginger
3 garlic cloves
1 tablespoon coriander seeds
2 teaspoons ground cumin
1 teaspoon cardamom pods
large pinch cayenne pepper
2 tablespoons ghee or oil
1 onion, extra, sliced
2 tablespoons tomato paste
(concentrated purée)
125 g (4½ oz/½ cup) plain yoghurt
spring onion (scallions), sliced, to garnish
steamed rice, to serve

SERVES 4–6

Remove all excess fat, skin and sinew from the lamb. Cut the meat into 3 cm (1¼ inch) cubes and put in a large bowl.

Put the onion, ginger, garlic, coriander seeds, cumin, cardamom pods, cayenne pepper and ½ teaspoon salt in a food processor and process until the mixture forms a smooth paste. Add the spice mixture to the lamb and mix well to coat. Set aside for 1 hour.

Heat the ghee in a large frying pan. Add the extra onion and cook, stirring, over medium-low heat until the onion is soft. Add the lamb mixture and cook for 8–10 minutes, stirring constantly, until the lamb cubes are browned all over. Add the tomato paste and 2 tablespoons of the yoghurt, and stir until combined. Simmer, uncovered, until the liquid has been absorbed. Add the remaining yoghurt, 2 tablespoons at a time, stirring until the mixture is nearly dry between each addition. Cover the pan and simmer over low heat for 30 minutes, or until the meat is tender, stirring occasionally. Add a little water if the mixture becomes too dry. Garnish with spring onion and serve with steamed rice.

PREPARATION TIME: 30 MINUTES +   COOKING TIME: 1 HOUR

MUSSELS WITH BLACK BEANS AND CORIANDER

1.5 kg (3 lb 5 oz) black mussels
1 tablespoon peanut oil
2 tablespoons black beans, rinsed and mashed
2 garlic cloves, finely chopped
1 teaspoon finely chopped fresh ginger
2 long red chillies, seeded and finely chopped
2 teaspoons finely chopped coriander (cilantro) leaves
1 tablespoon finely chopped coriander (cilantro) root
60 ml (2 fl oz/¼ cup) Chinese rice wine
2 tablespoons lime juice
2 teaspoons sugar
steamed rice, to serve

SERVES 4

Scrub the mussels with a stiff brush and pull out the hairy beards. Discard any broken mussels, or open ones that don't close when tapped on the bench. Rinse well.

Heat a wok until very hot, add the oil and swirl to coat the base and side. Add the black beans, garlic, ginger, chilli, 1 teaspoon coriander leaves and the coriander root, and cook over low heat for 2–3 minutes, or until fragrant. Pour in the rice wine and increase the heat to high. Add half the mussels in a single layer and cover with a tight-fitting lid. Cook for 2–3 minutes, or until the mussels have just opened. Discard any mussels that do not open. Remove from the wok, and repeat with the remaining mussels until all are cooked.

Transfer the mussels to a serving dish, leaving the cooking liquid in the wok. Add the lime juice, sugar and remaining coriander leaves to the wok and cook for 30 seconds. Pour the sauce over the mussels and serve with steamed rice.

PREPARATION TIME: 20 MINUTES   COOKING TIME: 10 MINUTES

SICHUAN CHICKEN

¼ teaspoon Chinese five-spice
750 g (1 lb 10 oz) boneless, skinless chicken thighs, halved
2 tablespoons peanut oil
1 tablespoon finely sliced fresh ginger
1 teaspoon chilli bean paste
1 teaspoon sichuan peppercorns, crushed
2 tablespoons light soy sauce
1 tablespoon Chinese rice wine
600 g (1 lb 5 oz) baby bok choy (pak choy), leaves separated
steamed rice, to serve

SERVES 4

Rub the Chinese five-spice over the chicken pieces. Heat a wok to very hot, add half the oil and swirl to coat the base and side. Add the chicken and cook for 2 minutes on each side, or until nicely browned. Remove from the wok.

Reduce the heat to medium. Add the ginger and cook for 30 seconds. Add the chilli bean paste and crushed peppercorns. Return the chicken to the wok then add the soy sauce, Chinese rice wine and 125 ml (4 fl oz/½ cup) water and simmer for 15–20 minutes, or until the chicken is cooked through.

Meanwhile, heat the remaining oil in a saucepan. Add the bok choy and toss gently and constantly for 1 minute, or until the leaves wilt and the stems are tender. Serve with the chicken and some steamed rice.

PREPARATION TIME: 10 MINUTES   COOKING TIME: 25 MINUTES

Mussels with black beans and coriander

THAI MUSAMAN BEEF CURRY

1 tablespoon tamarind pulp

125 ml (4 fl oz/½ cup) boiling water

2 tablespoons vegetable oil

750 g (1 lb 10 oz) lean stewing beef, cubed

500 ml (17 fl oz/2 cups) coconut milk

4 cardamom pods, bruised

500 ml (17 fl oz/2 cups) coconut cream

2 tablespoons ready-made Musaman
curry paste

2 tablespoons fish sauce

8 pickling onions (see Notes)

8 baby potatoes (see Notes)

2 tablespoons grated palm sugar

80 g (2¾ oz/½ cup) unsalted peanuts,
roasted and ground

SERVES 4

Put the tamarind pulp and boiling water in a bowl and set aside to cool. Mash the pulp with your fingertips to dissolve the pulp, then strain and reserve the liquid, and discard the pulp.

Heat a non-stick wok over high heat, add the oil and swirl to coat the base and side. Add the beef in batches and cook over high heat for 5 minutes, or until browned all over. Reduce the heat, add the coconut milk and cardamom pods, and simmer for 1 hour, or until the beef is tender. Remove the beef from the wok. Strain the cooking liquid into a bowl and reserve.

Heat the coconut cream in the cleaned wok and stir in the curry paste. Cook for 10 minutes, or until the oil starts to separate from the cream. Add the fish sauce, onions, potatoes, beef mixture, palm sugar, peanuts, tamarind water and the reserved cooking liquid. Simmer for about 30 minutes, or until the sauce has thickened and the meat is tender.

PREPARATION TIME: 30 MINUTES +   COOKING TIME: 2 HOURS

NOTES: It is important that the pickling onions and baby potatoes are small and similar in size to ensure that they cook evenly.

Also, use a non-stick or stainless steel wok as the tamarind purée will react with the metal in a regular wok and badly taint the dish.

BUTTER CHICKEN

2 tablespoons peanut oil

1 kg (2 lb 4 oz) boneless, skinless chicken thighs, quartered

60 g (2¼ oz) butter or ghee

2 teaspoons garam masala

2 teaspoons sweet paprika

2 teaspoons ground coriander

1 tablespoon finely chopped fresh ginger

¼ teaspoon chilli powder

1 cinnamon stick

6 cardamom pods, bruised

350 g (12 oz) tomato passata (puréed tomatoes)

1 tablespoon sugar

60 g (2¼ oz/¼ cup) plain yoghurt

125 ml (4 fl oz/½ cup) pouring (whipping) cream

1 tablespoon lemon juice

poppadoms, to serve

SERVES 4–6

Heat a wok to very hot, add 1 tablespoon oil and swirl to coat the base and side. Add half the chicken and stir-fry for about 4 minutes, or until nicely browned. Remove from the wok. Add a little extra oil, if needed, and brown the remaining chicken. Remove from the wok and set aside.

Reduce the heat to medium, add the butter and stir until melted. Add the garam masala, paprika, coriander, ginger, chilli powder, cinnamon stick and cardamom pods, and stir-fry for 1 minute, or until the spices are fragrant. Return the chicken to the wok and mix in until coated in the spices. Add the puréed tomatoes and sugar and simmer, stirring, for 15 minutes, or until the chicken is tender and the sauce is thick. Stir in the yoghurt, cream and lemon juice and simmer for 5 minutes, or until the sauce has thickened slightly. Serve with poppadoms.

PREPARATION TIME: 10 MINUTES   COOKING TIME: 35 MINUTES

BALINESE SEAFOOD CURRY

CURRY PASTE

2 tomatoes

5 small red chillies, seeded and chopped

5 garlic cloves, chopped

2 lemon grass stems, white part only, sliced

1 tablespoon coriander seeds, dry-roasted and ground

1 teaspoon shrimp powder, dry-roasted (see Notes)

1 tablespoon ground almonds

1/4 teaspoon ground nutmeg

1 teaspoon ground turmeric

3 tablespoons tamarind purée

400 g (14 oz) raw prawns (shrimp)

1 tablespoon lime juice

250 g (9 oz) swordfish, cut into 3 cm (1¼ inch) cubes

250 g (9 oz) calamari tubes, cut into 1 cm (½ inch) rings

60 ml (2 fl oz/¼ cup) vegetable oil

2 red onions, chopped

2 small red chillies, seeded and sliced

125 ml (4 fl oz/½ cup) fish stock

shredded Thai basil, to garnish

SERVES 6

To make the curry paste, score a cross in the base of each tomato. Put in a heatproof bowl and cover with boiling water. Leave for 30 seconds, then transfer to cold water, drain and peel away the skin from the cross. Cut the tomatoes in half, scoop out the seeds and chop the flesh. Put in a food processor with the remaining paste ingredients and blend until a thick paste forms.

Peel the prawns and gently pull out the dark vein from each prawn back, starting at the head end.

Pour the lime juice into a bowl and season. Add the fish, coat well and allow to marinate for 20 minutes.

Heat a non-stick wok over high heat, add the oil and swirl to coat the base and side. Add the onion, chilli and curry paste, and cook, stirring occasionally, over low heat for 10 minutes, or until fragrant. Add the swordfish and prawns, and stir to coat in the curry paste mixture. Cook for 3 minutes, or until the prawns just turn pink, then add the calamari and cook for a further 1 minute. Add the stock and bring to the boil, then reduce the heat and simmer for 2 minutes, or until the seafood is cooked and tender. Season to taste and garnish with the shredded fresh basil.

PREPARATION TIME: 20 MINUTES +   COOKING TIME: 20 MINUTES

NOTES: If you can't find shrimp powder, put some dried shrimp in a mortar and pestle or small food processor and grind or process into a fine powder.

Use a non-stick or stainless steel wok to cook this recipe as the tamarind will react with the metal in a regular wok and badly taint the dish.

MADRAS CURRY

1 kg (2 lb 4 oz) skirt or chuck steak
1 tablespoon ground coriander
1½ tablespoons ground cumin
1 teaspoon brown mustard seeds
½ teaspoon cracked black peppercorns
1 teaspoon chilli powder
1 teaspoon ground turmeric
2 teaspoons crushed garlic
2 teaspoons grated fresh ginger
2–3 tablespoons white vinegar
1 tablespoon oil or ghee
1 onion, chopped
60 g (2¼ oz/¼ cup) tomato paste
(concentrated purée)
250 ml (9 fl oz/1 cup) beef stock
steamed rice, to serve

SERVES 4

Trim the excess fat and sinew from the meat, and cut it into 2.5 cm (1 inch) cubes.

Put the coriander, cumin, mustard seeds, peppercorns, chilli powder, turmeric, garlic, ginger and 1 teaspoon salt in a small bowl and stir to combine. Add the vinegar and mix to a smooth paste.

Heat the oil in a large frying pan. Add the onion and cook over medium heat until just soft. Add the spice paste and stir for 1 minute. Add the meat and cook, stirring, until it is coated with the spice paste. Add the tomato paste and stock. Simmer, covered, for about 1 hour 30 minutes, or until the meat is tender. Serve with steamed rice.

PREPARATION TIME: 20 MINUTES   COOKING TIME: 1 HOUR 30 MINUTES

MILD VIETNAMESE CHICKEN CURRY

125 g (4½ oz) dried rice vermicelli
185 ml (6 fl oz/¾ cup) oil
4 large chicken quarters (leg and thigh), skin and excess fat removed, cut into thirds
1 tablespoon curry powder
1 teaspoon caster (superfine) sugar
80 ml (2½ fl oz/⅓ cup) vegetable oil
500 g (1 lb 2 oz) orange sweet potato, peeled, cut into 3 cm (1¼ inch) cubes
1 large onion, cut into thin wedges
4 garlic cloves, chopped
1 lemon grass stem, white part only, finely chopped
2 bay leaves
1 large carrot, cut diagonally into 1 cm (½ inch) pieces
400 ml (14 fl oz) coconut milk

SERVES 6

Break the vermicelli into short lengths. Heat half the oil in a wok over medium heat. Cook the vermicelli in batches until crisp, adding more oil when necessary. Drain on paper towel and set aside.

Pat the chicken dry with paper towel. Put the curry powder, sugar, ½ teaspoon black pepper and 2 teaspoons salt in a bowl, and mix together well. Rub the curry mixture onto the chicken pieces then place the chicken on a plate, cover with plastic wrap and refrigerate overnight.

Heat a wok over high heat, add the oil and swirl to coat the base and side. Add the sweet potato and cook over medium heat for 3 minutes, or until lightly golden. Remove with a slotted spoon and set aside.

Remove all but 2 tablespoons of the oil from the wok. Add the onion and cook, stirring, for 5 minutes. Add the garlic, lemon grass and bay leaves, and cook for 2 minutes. Add the chicken and cook, stirring, over medium heat for 5 minutes, or until well coated in the mixture and starting to change colour.

Add 250 ml (9 fl oz/1 cup) water and simmer, covered, over low heat for 20 minutes, stirring occasionally. Add the carrot, sweet potato and coconut milk, and simmer, uncovered, stirring occasionally, for 30 minutes, or until the chicken is cooked and tender. Be careful not to break up the sweet potato cubes. Serve with the crisp vermicelli.

PREPARATION TIME: 30 MINUTES +   COOKING TIME: 1 HOUR 10 MINUTES

JUNGLE CURRY PRAWNS

600 g (1 lb 5 oz) raw prawns (shrimp)
1 tablespoon peanut oil
1 garlic clove, crushed
60 g (2¼ oz/¼ cup) jungle curry paste (see Note)
1 tablespoon fish sauce
30 g (1 oz) ground candlenuts
300 ml (10½ fl oz) fish stock
1 tablespoon whisky
3 makrut (kaffir lime) leaves, torn
1 small carrot, quartered lengthways and thinly sliced on the diagonal
150 g (5½ oz) snake (yard-long) beans, cut into 2 cm (¾ inch) lengths
50 g (1¾ oz) tinned bamboo shoots, sliced
Thai basil, to garnish
steamed rice, to serve

SERVES 6

Peel the prawns and gently pull out the dark vein from each prawn back, starting at the head end.

Heat a wok over medium heat, add the oil and swirl to coat the base and side. Add the garlic and curry paste and cook, stirring, for 5 minutes. Add the fish sauce, ground candlenuts, fish stock, whisky, makrut leaves, prawns, carrot, beans and bamboo shoots. Bring to the boil then reduce the heat and simmer for 5 minutes, or until cooked. Garnish with the basil then serve with steamed rice.

PREPARATION TIME: 20 MINUTES   COOKING TIME: 10 MINUTES

NOTE: Jungle curry paste is available from Asian grocery stores and some supermarkets. You can use any green curry paste as a substitute.

PANANG BEEF

CURRY PASTE

8-10 large dried red chillies
6 red Asian shallots, chopped
6 garlic cloves, chopped
1 teaspoon ground coriander
1 tablespoon ground cumin
1 teaspoon white pepper
2 lemon grass stems, white part only, bruised, sliced
1 tablespoon chopped fresh galangal
6 coriander (cilantro) roots
2 teaspoons shrimp paste
2 tablespoons roasted peanuts

400 ml (14 fl oz) tinned coconut cream (do not shake)
1 kg (2 lb 4 oz) round or blade steak, cut into 1 cm (½ inch) slices
400 ml (14 fl oz) tinned coconut milk
90 g (3¼ oz/⅓ cup) crunchy peanut butter
4 makrut (kaffir lime) leaves
60 ml (2 fl oz/¼ cup) lime juice
2½ tablespoons fish sauce
3-4 tablespoons grated palm sugar (jaggery)
steamed rice, to serve
chopped roasted peanuts, to garnish
Thai basil, to garnish

SERVES 4-6

To make the curry paste, put the chillies in a bowl and cover with boiling water. Soak for 20 minutes, or until softened. Remove the seeds and roughly chop the flesh. Put the chopped chillies in a food processor along with the shallots, garlic, ground coriander, ground cumin, white pepper, lemon grass, galangal, coriander roots, shrimp paste and roasted peanuts and process until a smooth paste forms. You might need to add a little water if the paste is too thick.

Open the tin of coconut cream and scoop off the really thick cream from the top. Put this thick cream in a wok and cook over medium heat for 10 minutes, or until the oil starts to separate from the cream. Stir in 8 tablespoons of the curry paste and cook, stirring often, for 5-8 minutes, or until fragrant. Add the beef, coconut milk, peanut butter, makrut leaves and the remaining coconut cream to the wok and cook for 8 minutes, or until the beef just starts to change colour. Reduce the heat to low and simmer for 30 minutes, or until the beef is tender, stirring every few minutes to prevent it from catching on the bottom. Stir in the lime juice, fish sauce and sugar until they are mixed into the curry. Serve with steamed rice and garnish with the roasted peanuts and basil.

PREPARATION TIME: 30 MINUTES +   COOKING TIME: 1 HOUR

NOTE: Panang curry and Musaman curry are the two Thai curries with the most similarities to Indian curries. The similarity is due to the inclusion of many of the same dried spices. The heavier spice flavours of these two curries are traceable to Muslim origins in the south of Thailand. It is these same spices that make them more suitable to be made with red meats, such as beef or lamb, than poultry or seafood.

BALTI LAMB

1 kg (2 lb 4 oz) lamb leg steaks, cut into 3 cm (1¼ inch) cubes
5 tablespoons ready-made Balti curry paste
1 litre (35 fl oz/4 cups) boiling water
2 tablespoons ghee or vegetable oil
1 large onion, finely chopped
3 garlic cloves, crushed
1 tablespoon garam masala
2 tablespoons chopped coriander (cilantro) leaves, plus extra, to garnish
poppadoms, to serve
steamed rice, to serve

SERVES 4

Put the lamb, 1 tablespoon of the curry paste and the boiling water in a wok and mix together. Bring to the boil over high heat then reduce the heat to very low and cook, covered, for 40–50 minutes, or until the meat is almost cooked through. Drain, set the meat aside, and reserve the sauce.

Heat the ghee in a clean wok over medium heat. Add the onion and cook for 5–7 minutes, or until soft. Add the garlic and garam masala and cook for a further 2–3 minutes. Increase the heat, add the remaining curry paste and return the lamb to the wok. Cook for 5 minutes, or until the meat has browned. Slowly add the reserved sauce and simmer over low heat, stirring occasionally, for 15 minutes. Add the chopped coriander leaves and 250 ml (9 fl oz/1 cup) water and simmer for 15 minutes, or until the meat is tender and the sauce has thickened slightly. Season to taste.

Garnish with the extra coriander leaves and serve with poppadoms and steamed rice.

PREPARATION TIME: 15 MINUTES   COOKING TIME: 1 HOUR 25 MINUTES

NASI LEMAK

RENDANG

2 onions, roughly chopped

2 garlic cloves, crushed

400 ml (14 fl oz) tinned coconut milk

2 teaspoons ground coriander

½ teaspoon ground fennel

2 teaspoons ground cumin

¼ teaspoon ground cloves

1.5 kg (3 lb 5 oz) chuck steak, cut into cubes

4–6 small red chillies, chopped

1 tablespoon lemon juice

1 lemon grass stem, white part only, bruised and cut lengthways

2 teaspoons grated palm sugar (jaggery)

COCONUT RICE

300 g (10½ oz/1½ cups) long-grain rice

2 red Asian shallots

2 slices ginger

pinch fenugreek seeds

2 pandanus leaves, knotted

400 ml (14 fl oz) tinned coconut milk

SAMBAL IKAN BILIS

60 ml (2 fl oz/¼ cup) oil

5 red Asian shallots, sliced

2 garlic cloves, crushed

1 lemon grass stem, white part only, thinly sliced

½ teaspoon shrimp paste

2 tablespoons chilli paste

100 g (3½ oz) ikan bilis, soaked and washed (see Note)

1 teaspoon sugar

2 tablespoons lime juice

SERVES 4

To make the rendang, put the onion, garlic and 1 tablespoon of water into a food processor and blend to form a smooth paste.

Pour the coconut milk into a wok and bring to the boil, then reduce the heat to medium and cook, stirring occasionally, for 15 minutes, or until the milk is reduced by half and the oil has separated. Do not allow the milk to brown. Add the coriander, fennel, cumin and cloves to the wok and stir for 1 minute. Add the meat and cook for 2 minutes, or until it browns. Add the chilli, lemon juice, lemon grass, sugar and prepared rendang mixture. Cook, covered, over medium heat for about 2 hours, or until the liquid is reduced and thickened. Stir often. Remove the cover and continue cooking until the oil separates again. Take care not to burn the sauce. The curry is cooked when it is brown and dry.

Meanwhile, to make the coconut rice, put the rice, shallots, ginger, fenugreek, pandanus leaves and 1 teaspoon salt in a saucepan. Pour enough coconut milk over the rice so there is 2 cm (¾ inch) of liquid above the surface of the rice. Cover and cook until dry, then remove the pandanus leaf, sprinkle the rest of the coconut milk over the rice, then fluff up the grains. Stand for 15 minutes, until the coconut milk is completely absorbed.

To make the sambal, heat the oil in a wok, add the shallots, garlic, lemon grass, shrimp paste and chilli paste, and stir-fry until fragrant. Add the ikan bilis and stir-fry for a few more minutes. Mix in the sugar and lime juice. Serve with the rendang and rice.

PREPARATION TIME: 40 MINUTES +   COOKING TIME: 2 HOURS 40 MINUTES

NOTE: Ikan bilis are dried anchovies. In Malaysia, nasi lemak is traditionally served for breakfast.

NORTH VIETNAMESE BRAISED PORK LEG

1½ tablespoons vegetable oil

1 kg (2 lb 4 oz) boned pork leg in one piece, skin and fat intact

1 teaspoon shrimp paste

5 garlic cloves, crushed

3 red Asian shallots, finely chopped

3 teaspoons ground galangal

1 teaspoon ground turmeric

2 teaspoons sugar

2 tablespoons fish sauce

500 ml (17 fl oz/2 cups) beef stock diluted with 200 ml (7 fl oz) water

2 tablespoons Chinese black vinegar

1 teaspoon cornflour (cornstarch)

3 spring onions (scallions), thinly sliced

SERVES 4–6

Heat a wok to very hot, add 2 teaspoons of the oil and swirl to coat the base and side. Put the pork in the wok, skin side down, and cook for 2 minutes until well browned. Turn and cook the other side for a further 2 minutes, or until browned. Remove and set aside to cool. Cut the pork into 3 cm (1¼ inch) cubes.

Preheat the grill (broiler) to high, wrap the shrimp paste in foil, and put under the hot grill for 5 minutes. Cool, remove the foil, then put the paste in a large bowl with the garlic, shallots, galangal, turmeric, sugar and fish sauce and mix well. Add the pork to the bowl and coat it in the marinade. Cover and refrigerate for 1–2 hours.

Heat the wok until hot, add the remaining oil, and swirl to coat the base and side. Add the pork and stir-fry in batches for 1–2 minutes, or until browned. Pour in the stock and vinegar, and simmer, covered, over low heat for 1½ hours, or until very tender. Skim the surface constantly to remove any fat and scum that floats to the surface.

Dissolve the cornflour in 1 teaspoon water. Remove the pork from the liquid with a slotted spoon and set aside. Bring the remaining stock to a simmer and skim the surface. Mix in the cornflour paste. Simmer for 2 minutes, or until thickened, then return the pork to the wok and add the spring onion. Season and serve.

PREPARATION TIME: 30 MINUTES +   COOKING TIME: 1 HOUR 45 MINUTES

FISH BALL CURRY

1 large onion, chopped
1 teaspoon sambal oelek
1 tablespoon finely chopped fresh ginger
1 lemon grass stem, white part only, finely chopped
3 tablespoons chopped coriander (cilantro) roots
½ teaspoon ground cardamom
1 tablespoon tomato paste (concentrated purée)
1 tablespoon vegetable oil
1 tablespoon fish sauce
500 ml (17 fl oz/2 cups) coconut milk
24 fish balls (if frozen, thawed) (see Note)
2 teaspoons lime juice
3 tablespoons chopped coriander (cilantro), plus, extra, to garnish
steamed rice, to serve

SERVES 6

Put the onion, sambal oelek, ginger, lemon grass, coriander, cardamom and tomato paste in a food processor, and blend to form a smooth paste.

Heat a wok over medium heat, add the oil and swirl to coat the base and side. Add the paste and cook, stirring, over medium heat for 4 minutes, or until fragrant. Stir in the fish sauce, coconut milk and 250 ml (9 fl oz/1 cup) water. Bring to the boil and cook for 5 minutes, then reduce the heat and simmer for a further 5 minutes, or until the sauce has reduced and thickened slightly.

Add the fish balls and lime juice and cook for 2 minutes. Do not overcook or the fish balls will be tough and rubbery. Stir in the coriander and garnish with extra coriander. Serve with steamed rice.

PREPARATION TIME: 20 MINUTES   COOKING TIME: 20 MINUTES

NOTE: Fish balls are available from the refrigerated section of large supermarkets and Asian grocery stores.

DHAL

250 g (9 oz/1 cup) red lentils
4 cm (1½ inch) piece ginger, cut into 3 slices
½ teaspoon ground turmeric
3 tablespoons ghee or oil
2 garlic cloves, crushed
1 onion, finely chopped
pinch asafoetida (optional)
1 teaspoon cumin seeds
1 teaspoon ground coriander
¼ teaspoon chilli powder
1 tablespoon chopped coriander (cilantro) leaves

SERVES 4–6

Place the lentils and 1 litre (35 fl oz/4 cups) water in a saucepan over medium heat and bring to the boil. Reduce the heat to low, add the ginger and turmeric, and simmer, covered, for 1 hour or until the lentils are tender. Stir every 5 minutes during the last 30 minutes to prevent the lentils sticking to the pan. Remove the ginger and stir in ½ teaspoon salt.

Meanwhile, heat the ghee in a frying pan. Add the garlic and onion, and cook over medium heat for 3 minutes, or until the onion is golden. Add the asafoetida, if using, cumin seeds, ground coriander and chilli powder, and cook for 2 minutes.

Add the onion mixture and fresh coriander to the lentils and stir gently to combine. Serve immediately.

PREPARATION TIME: 15 MINUTES   COOKING TIME: 1 HOUR

PORK VINDALOO

1 kg (2 lb 4 oz) pork fillets
60 ml (2 fl oz/¼ cup) vegetable oil
2 onions, finely chopped
4 garlic cloves, finely chopped
1 tablespoon finely chopped ginger
1 tablespoon garam masala
2 teaspoons brown mustard seeds
4 tablespoons ready-made vindaloo curry paste
1 tablespoon white vinegar
steamed rice, to serve
poppadoms, to serve

SERVES 4

Trim the pork of any excess fat and sinew and cut into bite-sized pieces.

Heat a wok over medium heat, add the oil and swirl to coat the base and side. Add the meat in small batches and cook for 5–7 minutes, or until browned. Remove from the wok.

Add the onion, garlic, ginger, garam masala and mustard seeds to the wok, and cook, stirring, for 5 minutes, or until the onion is soft. Add the vindaloo paste and cook for 2 minutes.

Return all the meat to the wok, add 750 ml (26 fl oz/3 cups) water and bring to the boil. Reduce the heat and simmer, covered, for 1½ hours, or until the meat is tender. Stir in the vinegar 15 minutes before serving and season to taste with salt. Serve with steamed rice and poppadoms.

PREPARATION TIME: 20 MINUTES   COOKING TIME: 1 HOUR 45 MINUTES

MALAYSIAN FISH HEAD CURRY

CURRY PASTE
4 garlic cloves, chopped
4 red Asian shallots, chopped
1 lemon grass stem, white part only,
finely chopped
3 cm (1¼ inch) piece fresh galangal,
finely chopped
2 large red chillies, chopped

400 ml (14 fl oz) tinned coconut cream
(do not shake)
10 curry leaves
2 tablespoons Malaysian seafood curry
powder
½ teaspoon ground turmeric
500 ml (17 fl oz/2 cups) fish stock
2 tablespoons tamarind purée
2 tablespoons fish sauce
1 tablespoon sugar
200 g (7 oz) eggplant (aubergine), cut into
1 cm (½ inch) slices
150 g (5½ oz) okra, cut into
1 cm (½ inch) slices
four 200 g (7 oz) fish heads (ask your
fishmonger to clean and scale them)
2 ripe tomatoes, cut into eighths
2 large green chillies, cut into
1 cm (½ inch) slices
steamed rice, to serve

SERVES 6

To make the curry paste, put all the ingredients in a food processor or blender and blend to a smooth paste, adding a little water if needed.

Lift the thick cream off the top of the coconut cream. Put the cream in a non-stick wok and bring to the boil. Simmer for 10 minutes, or until the oil starts to separate from the cream. Add the curry paste and cook for 5 minutes, or until fragrant. Add the curry leaves, curry powder and turmeric and cook for 1 minute.

Stir in the stock, tamarind purée, fish sauce, sugar and remaining coconut cream and bring to the boil for 1 minute. Add the eggplant and okra, reduce the heat and simmer for 15 minutes. Add the fish heads and cook for a further 5 minutes, turning to cook evenly. Stir in the tomato and green chilli until heated through; the vegetables should be tender and the fish eyes opaque. Season to taste and serve with steamed rice.

PREPARATION TIME: 20 MINUTES   COOKING TIME: 40 MINUTES

SAAG PANEER

2 litres (70 fl oz/8 cups) milk
80 ml (2½ fl oz/⅓ cup) lemon juice
100 g (3½ oz/⅓ cup) plain yoghurt
500 g (1 lb 2 oz) spinach
2 garlic cloves
2 cm (¾ inch) piece fresh ginger, grated
2 green chillies, chopped
1 onion, chopped
2 tablespoons ghee or oil
1 teaspoon ground cumin
½ teaspoon freshly grated nutmeg
125 ml (4 fl oz/½ cup) pouring (whipping) cream

SERVES 4

Heat the milk in a large saucepan until just boiling. Reduce the heat, add the lemon juice and 2 tablespoons yoghurt, and stir until the mixture begins to curdle. Remove the pan from the heat and allow the milk mixture to stand for 5 minutes or until curds start to form.

Line a colander with muslin (cheesecloth). Pour the curd mixture into the colander and leave until most of the liquid has drained away. Gather up the corners of the muslin, hold them together and squeeze as much moisture as possible from the curd. Return the muslin-wrapped curd to the colander and leave in a cool place for 3 hours until the curd is very firm and all the whey has drained away. Cut the cheese into 4 cm (1½ inch) cubes.

Steam the spinach over simmering water until tender. Squeeze out any excess moisture and chop finely.

Place the garlic, ginger, chilli and onion in a food processor and process to form a paste.

Heat the ghee in a wok, add the paste and cook over medium heat for 5 minutes, or until the ghee begins to separate from the paste. Add the cumin, nutmeg, remaining yoghurt, 1 teaspoon salt and 250 ml (9 fl oz/1 cup) water and simmer for 5 minutes. Transfer the mixture to a food processor, add the steamed spinach and process until smooth.

Return the mixture to the wok, add the chopped cheese and cream, and cook for 10 minutes or until the sauce is heated through.

PREPARATION TIME: 20 MINUTES +   COOKING TIME: 30 MINUTES

CLAY POT CHICKEN AND VEGETABLES

500 g (1 lb 2 oz) boneless, skinless
chicken thighs
1 tablespoon soy sauce
1 tablespoon dry sherry
6 dried Chinese mushrooms
2 tablespoons peanut oil
2 small leeks, white part only, sliced
5 cm (2 inch) piece ginger, grated
125 ml (4 fl oz/½ cup) chicken stock
1 teaspoon sesame oil
250 g (9 oz) orange sweet potato, sliced
3 teaspoons cornflour (cornstarch)
steamed rice, to serve

SERVES 4

Wash the chicken under cold water and pat it dry with paper towel. Cut the chicken into small pieces. Put it in a dish with the soy sauce and sherry, cover and marinate for 30 minutes in the refrigerator.

Cover the mushrooms with hot water and soak for 20 minutes. Drain and squeeze to remove any excess liquid. Remove the stems and chop the caps into shreds.

Drain the chicken, reserving the marinade. Heat half the oil in a wok, swirling gently to coat the base and side. Add half the chicken pieces and stir-fry briefly until seared on all sides. Transfer the chicken to a flameproof clay pot or casserole dish. Stir-fry the remaining chicken and add it to the clay pot.

Heat the remaining oil in the wok. Add the leek and ginger and stir-fry for 1 minute. Add the mushrooms, remaining marinade, stock and sesame oil and cook for 2 minutes. Transfer to the clay pot with the sweet potato and cook, covered, on the top of the stove over very low heat for about 20 minutes.

Dissolve the cornflour in a little water and add it to the pot. Cook, stirring over high heat, until the mixture boils and thickens. Serve the chicken and vegetables at once with steamed rice.

PREPARATION TIME: 20 MINUTES +   COOKING TIME: 25 MINUTES

NOTE: Like all stews, this is best cooked 1–2 days ahead and stored, covered, in the refrigerator to allow the flavours to mature. It can also be frozen, but omit the sweet potato. Steam or boil the potato separately when the dish is reheating and stir it through.

INDIAN PRAWN CURRY

1 kg (2 lb 4 oz) raw prawns (shrimp)
25 g (1 oz) ghee or butter
1 onion, finely chopped
3 garlic cloves, crushed
1 teaspoon grated fresh ginger
½ teaspoon cayenne pepper
2 teaspoons ground cumin
1 teaspoon garam masala
½ teaspoon ground turmeric
425 g (15 oz) tinned chopped tomatoes
80 ml (2½ fl oz/⅓ cup) coconut cream
2 teaspoons finely chopped green chilli
2 tablespoons chopped coriander
(cilantro)

SERVES 4

Peel the prawns and gently pull out the dark vein from each prawn back, starting at the head end.

Heat the ghee or butter in a wok over medium heat. Add the onion and cook for 3 minutes, or until soft and golden. Add the garlic and ginger and cook for 1 minute. Add the cayenne pepper, cumin, garam masala and turmeric and cook for 1 minute, or until fragrant. Add the prawns and tomato and simmer for 10–15 minutes, or until the prawns are cooked and the liquid has reduced. Stir in the coconut cream. Add the chilli a little at a time until the mixture is as hot as you like. Season to taste, and serve scattered with coriander.

PREPARATION TIME: 25 MINUTES   COOKING TIME: 20 MINUTES

NOTE: You can substitute white fish fillets for half or all the prawns.

SWEET KECAP PORK

500 g (1 lb 2 oz) pork, diced
2 tablespoons oil
1 large onion, finely chopped
3 garlic cloves, finely chopped
5 cm (2 inch) piece ginger, grated
3 red chillies, finely chopped
2 tablespoons kecap manis
250 ml (9 fl oz/1 cup) coconut milk
2 teaspoons lime juice
red chilli, finely sliced, to serve
steamed rice, to serve

SERVES 4

Mix together the pork, oil and 1/4 teaspoon each of salt and pepper and leave to stand for 10 minutes.

Heat a wok or heavy-based frying pan and cook the pork in several batches over medium heat, until well browned. Remove all the meat from the wok and set aside. Reduce the heat to low, add the onion, garlic, ginger and chilli and cook for 10 minutes, stirring occasionally until the onion is very soft and golden. Add the pork, kecap manis and coconut milk, and cook over low heat for 1 hour, stirring occasionally. Stir in the lime juice and serve with the chilli and steamed rice.

PREPARATION TIME: 20 MINUTES   COOKING TIME: 1 HOUR 10 MINUTES

CHICKEN KAPITAN

30 g (1 oz) small dried shrimp
80 ml (2½ fl oz/⅓ cup) oil
4-8 red chillies, seeded and finely chopped
4 garlic cloves, finely chopped
3 lemon grass stems (white part only), finely chopped
2 teaspoons ground turmeric
10 candlenuts
2 large onions, chopped
500 g (1 lb 2 oz) boneless, skinless chicken thighs, chopped
250 ml (9 fl oz/1 cup) coconut milk
125 ml (4 fl oz/½ cup) coconut cream
2 tablespoons lime juice
steamed rice, to serve

SERVES 4–6

Put the shrimp in a clean frying pan and dry-fry over low heat, shaking the pan regularly, for 3 minutes, or until the shrimp are dark orange and are giving off a strong aroma. Transfer the shrimp to a mortar and pestle and pound until finely ground. Set aside.

Put half the oil with the chilli, garlic, lemon grass, turmeric and candlenuts in a food processor and process in short bursts until very finely chopped, regularly scraping down the sides of the bowl with a rubber spatula.

Heat the remaining oil in a wok or frying pan, add the onion and ¼ teaspoon salt and cook over low heat for 8 minutes, or until golden, stirring regularly. Take care not to let the onion burn. Add the spice mixture and nearly all the ground shrimp meat, setting a little aside to use as garnish. Stir for 5 minutes. If the mixture begins to stick to the bottom of the pan, add 2 tablespoons coconut milk to the mixture. It is important to cook the mixture thoroughly to develop the flavours.

Add the chicken to the wok and stir well. Cook for 5 minutes, or until the chicken begins to brown. Stir in the remaining coconut milk and 250 ml (9 fl oz/1 cup) water, and bring to the boil. Reduce the heat and simmer for 7 minutes, or until the chicken is cooked and the sauce is thick. Add the coconut cream and bring the mixture back to the boil, stirring constantly. Add the lime juice and serve immediately, sprinkled lightly with the reserved ground shrimp meat. Serve with steamed rice.

PREPARATION TIME: 35 MINUTES   COOKING TIME: 30 MINUTES

BRAISED DUCK WITH MUSHROOMS

15 g (½ oz) dried Chinese mushrooms
1.5 kg (3 lb 5 oz) whole duck
2 teaspoons oil
2 tablespoons soy sauce
2 tablespoons Chinese rice wine
2 teaspoons sugar
2 wide strips orange peel
125 g (4½ oz) watercress

SERVES 6

Soak the mushrooms in hot water for 20 minutes. Drain well, discard the stems and thinly slice the caps.

Using a large heavy knife or cleaver, chop the duck into small pieces, cutting through the bone. Arrange the pieces on a rack and pour boiling water over them — the water will plump up the skin and help keep the duck succulent. Drain and pat dry with paper towel.

Heat the oil in a wok over medium heat and add the duck. Cook, in batches, for about 8 minutes, turning regularly, until browned. (The darker the browning at this stage, the better the colour when finished.) Between each batch, wipe out the pan with crumpled paper towel to remove excess oil.

Wipe the pan with paper towel again and return all the duck to the pan. Add the mushrooms, soy sauce, wine, sugar and orange peel. Bring the mixture to the boil, reduce the heat, cover and simmer gently for 35 minutes or until the duck is tender. Season to taste and stand for 10 minutes, covered, before serving.

Remove the duck from the sauce and discard the orange peel. Pick off small sprigs of the watercress and arrange them on one side of a large serving platter. Carefully place the duck segments on the other side of the plate — try not to place the duck on the watercress as it will become soggy. Carefully spoon a little of the sauce over the duck and serve.

PREPARATION TIME: 20 MINUTES +   COOKING TIME: 1 HOUR 10 MINUTES

NOTE: Braising the duck over low heat produces tender, melt-in-the-mouth meat and a delicious sauce. If the heat is too high, the duck will dry out and lose its flavour.

YELLOW VEGETABLE CURRY

YELLOW CURRY PASTE
8 small dried red chillies
1 teaspoon black peppercorns
2 teaspoons coriander seeds
2 teaspoons cumin seeds
1 teaspoon ground turmeric
1½ tablespoons chopped fresh galangal
5 garlic cloves, chopped
1 teaspoon grated fresh ginger
5 red Asian shallots, chopped
2 lemon grass stems, white part only, chopped
1 teaspoon shrimp paste
1 teaspoon finely chopped lime zest

2 tablespoons peanut oil
500 ml (17 fl oz/2 cups) coconut cream
125 ml (4 fl oz/½ cup) vegetable stock
150 g (5½ oz) snake (yard-long) beans, cut into 3 cm (1¼ inch) lengths
150 g (5½ oz) baby corn
1 slender eggplant (aubergine), cut into 1 cm (½ inch) slices
100 g (3½ oz) cauliflower, cut into small florets
2 small zucchini (courgettes), cut into 1 cm (½ inch) slices
1 small red capsicum (pepper), seeded, membrane removed and cut into 1 cm (½ inch) slices
1½ tablespoons fish sauce
1 teaspoon grated palm sugar (jaggery)
chopped red chilli, to garnish
coriander (cilantro) leaves, to garnish

SERVES 4

To make the curry paste, soak the chillies in boiling water for about 20 minutes. Drain and chop. Heat a frying pan, add the peppercorns, coriander seeds, cumin seeds and turmeric and dry-fry over medium heat for 3 minutes. Transfer to a mortar and pestle or food processor and finely grind. Put the ground spices, chilli, galangal, garlic, ginger, shallots, lemon grass and shrimp paste in a mortar and pestle and pound until smooth. Stir in the lime zest.

Heat a wok over medium heat, add the oil and swirl to coat the base and side. Add 2 tablespoons of the curry paste and cook for 1 minute. Add 250 ml (9 fl oz/1 cup) of the coconut cream. Bring to the boil, then simmer for 10 minutes, or until the liquid becomes thick and the oil starts to separate from the cream. Add the stock, vegetables and remaining coconut cream and cook for 5 minutes, or until the vegetables are tender. Stir in the fish sauce and sugar. Garnish with chilli and coriander.

PREPARATION TIME: 20 MINUTES +   COOKING TIME: 20 MINUTES

NONYA LIME CHICKEN

CURRY PASTE
70 g (2½ oz/⅔ cup) red Asian shallots
4 garlic cloves
2 lemon grass stems, white part only,
chopped
2 teaspoons finely chopped fresh galangal
1 teaspoon ground turmeric
2 tablespoons sambal oelek
1 tablespoon shrimp paste

60 ml (2 fl oz/¼ cup) vegetable oil
1 kg (2 lb 4 oz) boneless, skinless chicken
thighs, cut into 3 cm (1¼ inch) cubes
400 ml (14 fl oz) coconut milk
1 teaspoon finely grated lime zest
125 ml (4 fl oz/½ cup) lime juice
6 makrut (kaffir lime) leaves, finely
shredded, plus extra, to garnish
2 tablespoons tamarind purée
steamed rice, to serve
lime wedges, to garnish

SERVES 4–6

Combine the curry paste ingredients in a food processor or blender and blend until a smooth paste forms.

Heat a non-stick wok until very hot, add the oil and swirl to coat the base and side. Add the curry paste and stir-fry for 1–2 minutes, or until fragrant. Add the chicken and stir-fry for 5 minutes, or until browned. Add the coconut milk, lime zest and juice, makrut leaves and tamarind purée. Reduce the heat and simmer for 15 minutes, or until the chicken is cooked and the sauce has reduced and thickened slightly. Season well with salt. Serve with steamed rice and garnish with lime wedges and the extra makrut leaves.

PREPARATION TIME: 20 MINUTES   COOKING TIME: 25 MINUTES

LAMB KOFTA

1 kg (2 lb 4 oz) minced (ground) lamb
1 onion, finely chopped
2 green chillies, finely chopped
3 teaspoons grated fresh ginger
3 garlic cloves, crushed
1 teaspoon ground cardamom
1 egg
25 g (1 oz/⅓ cup) fresh breadcrumbs
2 tablespoons ghee or oil

SAUCE
1 tablespoon ghee or oil
1 onion, sliced
1 green chilli, finely chopped
3 teaspoons grated fresh ginger
2 garlic cloves, crushed
1 teaspoon ground turmeric
3 teaspoons ground coriander
2 teaspoons ground cumin
1 teaspoon chilli powder
2 tablespoons white vinegar
185 g (6½ oz/¾ cup) plain yoghurt
310 ml (10¾ fl oz/1¼ cups) coconut milk
steamed rice, to serve

SERVES 4–6

Line a baking tray with baking paper. Place the minced lamb in a large bowl. Add the onion, chilli, ginger, garlic, cardamom, egg and breadcrumbs, and season well. Mix until combined. Roll level tablespoons of the mixture into balls, and place them on the prepared tray.

Heat the ghee in a frying pan, add the meatballs in two batches and cook over medium heat for 5 minutes at a time, or until browned all over. Transfer the meatballs to a large bowl.

To make the sauce, heat the ghee in the cleaned frying pan, add the onion, chilli, ginger, garlic and turmeric, and cook, stirring, over low heat until the onion is soft. Add the coriander, cumin, chilli powder, vinegar, meatballs and 350 ml (12 fl oz/1⅓ cups) water and stir gently. Cover and simmer for 30 minutes. Stir in the combined yoghurt and coconut milk and simmer for another 10 minutes with the pan partially covered. Serve with steamed rice.

PREPARATION TIME: 25 MINUTES   COOKING TIME: 50 MINUTES

SRI LANKAN FISH FILLETS IN TOMATO CURRY

60 ml (2 fl oz/¼ cup) lemon juice
60 ml (2 fl oz/¼ cup) coconut vinegar (see Note)
2 teaspoons cumin seeds
1 teaspoon ground turmeric
1 teaspoon cayenne pepper
1 kg (2 lb 4 oz) skinless, boneless firm white fish fillets
60 ml (2 fl oz/¼ cup) vegetable oil
1 large onion, finely chopped
3 large garlic cloves, crushed
2 tablespoons grated fresh ginger
1 teaspoon black mustard seeds
1.2 kg (2 lb 12 oz) tinned diced tomatoes
3 tablespoons finely chopped coriander (cilantro)
2 small green chillies, seeded and finely chopped
2 tablespoons grated palm sugar (jaggery)
steamed rice, to serve

SERVES 6

To make the marinade, put the lemon juice, coconut vinegar, cumin seeds, ground turmeric, cayenne pepper and 1 teaspoon salt in a shallow, non-metallic container and mix together thoroughly.

Carefully remove any remaining bones from the fish with tweezers and cut the flesh into 2.5 x 10 cm (1 x 4 inch) pieces. Add the fish pieces to the marinade and gently toss until they are well coated. Cover with plastic wrap and refrigerate for 30 minutes.

Heat a non-stick wok over high heat, add the oil and swirl to coat the base and side. Reduce the heat to low, add the onion, garlic, ginger and mustard seeds, and cook, stirring frequently, for 5 minutes. Add the fish and marinade, diced tomatoes, coriander, chilli and palm sugar to the wok and cover. Simmer gently, stirring occasionally, for 10–15 minutes, or until the fish is cooked and just flakes when tested with the tines of a fork. Serve with steamed rice.

PREPARATION TIME: 20 MINUTES +   COOKING TIME: 20 MINUTES

NOTE: Coconut vinegar is made from the sap of various palm trees.

SWEET AND STICKY

THAI STICKY RICE WITH MANGOES

400 g (14 oz/2 cups) long-grain white rice
1 tablespoon white sesame seeds
250 ml (9 fl oz/1 cup) coconut milk
70 g (2½ oz/½ cup) grated palm sugar (jaggery)
2–3 mangoes, peeled, seeded and sliced
60 ml (2 fl oz/¼ cup) coconut cream
mint sprigs, to garnish

SERVES 4

Put the rice in a sieve and wash under cold running water until the water runs clear. Put the rice in a glass or ceramic bowl, cover with water and soak overnight, or for at least 12 hours. Drain the rice.

Line a metal or bamboo steamer with a piece of muslin (cheesecloth). Put the rice on top of the muslin and cover the steamer with a tight-fitting lid. Put the steamer over a saucepan or wok of boiling water and steam over medium–low heat for 50 minutes, or until the rice is cooked. Replenish the pot with boiling water as necessary. Transfer the rice to a large bowl and fluff it up with a fork.

Toast the sesame seeds in a frying pan over medium heat for 3–4 minutes, shaking the pan gently until the seeds are golden brown. Remove from the pan immediately to prevent them burning.

Put the coconut milk into a small saucepan, then add the sugar and ¼ teaspoon salt. Slowly bring the mixture to the boil, stirring constantly until the sugar has dissolved. Reduce the heat and simmer for 5 minutes, or until the mixture is slightly thickened. Stir the mixture often while it is simmering, to prevent it sticking to the bottom of the pan.

Slowly pour the coconut milk over the top of the rice. Use a fork to lift and fluff up the rice. Do not stir the liquid through, otherwise the rice will become too gluggy. Let the rice mixture rest for 20 minutes before carefully spooning it into the centre of four warmed serving bowls. Arrange the mango slices on the rice mounds. Spoon a little coconut cream over the rice, sprinkle over the sesame seeds and garnish with the mint.

PREPARATION TIME: 10 MINUTES +   COOKING TIME: 1 HOUR 5 MINUTES

BANANA FRITTERS IN COCONUT BATTER

100 g (3½ oz) glutinous rice flour
100 g (3½ oz) freshly grated coconut
or 60 g (2¼ oz/⅔ cup) desiccated
coconut
55 g (2 oz/¼ cup) sugar
1 tablespoon sesame seeds
60 ml (2 fl oz/¼ cup) coconut milk
6 sugar bananas
oil, for deep-frying
vanilla ice cream, to serve
sesame seeds, toasted, extra, to garnish

SERVES 6

Combine the flour, coconut, sugar, sesame seeds, coconut milk and 60 ml (2 fl oz/¼ cup) water in a large bowl. Whisk to a smooth batter, adding more water if the batter is too thick. Set aside to rest for 1 hour.

Peel the bananas and cut in half lengthways (cut each portion in half again crossways if the bananas are large).

Fill a wok or large heavy-based saucepan one-third full of oil and heat to 180ºC (350ºF), or until a cube of bread dropped into the oil browns in 15 seconds. Dip each piece of banana into the batter then drop gently into the hot oil. Cook in batches for 4–6 minutes, or until golden brown all over. Remove with a slotted spoon and drain on crumpled paper towel. Serve hot with vanilla ice cream and a sprinkling of extra toasted sesame seeds.

PREPARATION TIME: 15 MINUTES +   COOKING TIME: 20 MINUTES

SAGO PUDDING

200 g (7 oz/1 cup) sago
185 g (6½ oz/1 cup) lightly packed soft
brown sugar
250 ml (9 fl oz/1 cup) coconut cream,
well chilled

SERVES 6

Soak the sago in 750 ml (26 fl oz/3 cups) water for 1 hour. Pour into a saucepan, add 2 tablespoons of the sugar and bring to the boil over low heat, stirring constantly. Reduce the heat and simmer, stirring occasionally, for 8 minutes. Cover and cook for 2–3 minutes, until the mixture becomes thick and the sago grains are translucent.

Half fill six wet 125 ml (4 fl oz/½ cup) moulds with the sago mixture. Refrigerate for 2 hours, or until set.

Combine the remaining sugar with 250 ml (9 fl oz/1 cup) water in a small saucepan and cook over low heat until the sugar dissolves. Simmer for 5–7 minutes, or until the syrup thickens. Remove from the heat and cool.

To serve, unmould the sago by wiping a cloth dipped in hot water over the mould and turn out onto the plate. Top with the sugar syrup and coconut cream.

PREPARATION TIME: 20 MINUTES +   TOTAL COOKING TIME: 20 MINUTES

Banana fritters in coconut batter

NEW YEAR SWEET DUMPLINGS

60 g (2¼ oz) black sesame paste, red bean paste or smooth peanut butter
80 g (2¾ oz/⅓ cup) caster (superfine) sugar
250 g (9 oz) glutinous rice flour
220 ml (7¾ fl oz) boiling water
30 g (1 oz) yellow rock sugar (see Note)

MAKES 24

Combine the sesame paste with the caster sugar in a small bowl.

Sift the rice flour into a bowl and stir in the boiling water. Knead carefully (the dough will be very hot) to form a soft, slightly sticky dough. Dust your hands with extra rice flour, roll the dough into a cylinder then divide it into cherry-size pieces. Cover the dough with a tea towel (dish towel) and, using one piece at a time, form each piece of dough into a flat round, then gather it into a cup shape. The dough should be fairly thin.

Fill each cup shape with 1 teaspoon of sesame paste and fold the top over, smoothing the dough so you have a round ball with no visible joins.

Bring 1 litre (35 fl oz/4 cups) water to the boil, add the rock sugar and stir until dissolved. Return to the boil, add the dumplings in batches and simmer for 5 minutes, or until they rise to the surface. Serve warm with a little of the syrup.

PREPARATION TIME: 40 MINUTES   COOKING TIME: 15 MINUTES

NOTE: Yellow rock sugar comes as uneven lumps of sugar, which may need to be further crushed before use if very big. It is a pure sugar that produces a clear syrup and makes sauces shiny and clear. You can use sugar cubes instead.

KHEER RICE PUDDING

65 g (2½ oz/⅓ cup) basmati rice
1.5 litres (52 fl oz/6 cups) milk
6 cardamom pods, lightly crushed
115 g (4 oz/½ cup) caster (superfine) sugar
40 g (1½ oz/¼ cup) chopped raisins
30 g (1 oz/¼ cup) slivered almonds
pinch of saffron threads
1 tablespoon rosewater (optional)
ground cinnamon (optional)

SERVES 4

Soak the rice in water for 30 minutes, then drain.

Pour the milk into a saucepan, add the cardamom pods and bring to the boil. Add the rice, reduce the heat and simmer for 1 hour, stirring often or until the rice is cooked. Add the sugar, raisins and slivered almonds, bring to a low boil and cook for 50 minutes, or until it is the consistency of porridge. Stir frequently to avoid sticking to the base of the pan. Remove the cardamom pods.

Mix the saffron threads with a little water and add to the mixture — just enough to give a pale yellow colour to the pudding. Stir in the rosewater, if using, when cooled. Serve warm or cold, with a sprinkling of cinnamon on top, if desired.

PREPARATION TIME: 15 MINUTES +   COOKING TIME: 1 HOUR 50 MINUTES

NOTE: Served at banquets, weddings and religious ceremonies, kheer is the 'Queen of desserts' or 'Queen of creams' in India, and is particularly popular in northern India. It is exotically delicious, rich and creamy, with the cardamom and almonds giving it a distinctive texture and flavour.

CARROT MILK PUDDING

1 litre (35 fl oz/4 cups) milk
235 g (8½ oz/1½ cups) grated carrot
40 g (1½ oz/⅓ cup) sultanas (golden raisins)
115 g (4 oz/½ cup) caster (superfine) sugar
¼ teaspoon ground cinnamon
¼ teaspoon ground cardamom
80 ml (2½ oz/⅓ cup) pouring (whipping) cream
2 tablespoons unsalted chopped pistachios

SERVES 6

Pour the milk into a large heavy-based saucepan and bring to the boil over medium heat, stirring often. Reduce the heat to low and simmer until reduced by half, stirring occasionally to prevent it from catching on the base of the pan. Add the carrot and sultanas and cook for a further 15 minutes. Add the sugar, cinnamon, cardamom and cream and cook, stirring, until the sugar has dissolved. Serve the pudding warm in small dishes, sprinkled with the pistachios.

PREPARATION TIME: 5 MINUTES   COOKING TIME: 1 HOUR

Kheer rice pudding

EGG TARTS

OUTER DOUGH

165 g (5³/4 oz/1¹/3 cups) plain (all-purpose) flour
2 tablespoons icing (confectioners') sugar
2 tablespoons oil

INNER DOUGH

125 g (4¹/2 oz/1 cup) plain (all-purpose) flour
100 g (3¹/2 oz) lard, chopped

CUSTARD

55 g (2 oz/¹/4 cup) caster (superfine) sugar
2 eggs

MAKES 18

To make the outer dough, sift the flour and icing sugar into a bowl. Make a well in the centre. Combine the oil with 80 ml (2¹/2 oz/¹/3 cup) water and pour into the dry ingredients. Mix with a flat-bladed knife, using a cutting action, to form a rough dough. (If the flour is very dry, add a little extra water.) Turn out onto a lightly floured surface and gather together in a smooth ball. Cover and set aside for 15 minutes.

To make the inner dough, sift the flour into a bowl. Using your fingertips, rub the lard into the flour until the mixture resembles breadcrumbs. Press the dough together into a ball, cover and set aside for 15 minutes.

On a lightly floured surface, roll the outer dough into a rectangle about 10 x 20 cm (4 x 8 inches). On a lightly floured surface, roll the inner dough into a smaller rectangle, one-third the size of the outer dough. Place the inner dough in the centre of the outer dough. Fold the outer dough over the inner dough so the short edges overlap and the inner dough is enclosed. Pinch the edges together to seal. Roll the dough away from you in one direction into a long rectangle, until it is about half as thick as it was previously. Fold the pastry into three layers by taking the left-hand edge over first, and then folding the right-hand edge on top. Wrap the dough in plastic wrap and refrigerate for 30 minutes. Preheat the oven to 210°C (415°F/Gas 6–7). Brush two 12-hole muffin tins with melted butter or oil.

To make the custard, place 80 ml (2¹/2 oz/¹/3 cup) water and the sugar in a saucepan and stir, without boiling, until the sugar dissolves. Bring to a boil and simmer, without stirring, for 1 minute. Cool the mixture for 5 minutes. Put the eggs in a bowl and beat lightly with a fork. Whisk the sugar syrup into the eggs until just combined. Strain.

Place the pastry on a lightly floured surface. With one open end towards you, roll the pastry out to a rectangle about 3 mm (¹/8 inch) thick. Cut out rounds of pastry using a 7 cm (2³/4 inch) fluted cutter. Carefully place the pastry rounds into the prepared patty pans. Fill each pastry case two-thirds full with the egg custard mixture. Bake for 15 minutes, or until just set. Be careful not to overcook the custard. Leave the egg tarts to cool for 3 minutes before removing them from the tin. Cool the tarts on a wire rack, and serve warm or cold.

PREPARATION TIME: 30 MINUTES +   COOKING TIME: 15 MINUTES

ALMOND JELLY

80 g (2³/₄ oz/¹/₃ cup) caster (superfine)
sugar
2 teaspoons agar-agar (see Note)
170 ml (5¹/₂ fl oz/²/₃ cup) evaporated milk
¹/₂ teaspoon natural almond extract
3 fresh mandarins, peeled and
segmented, or 300 g (10¹/₂ oz) fresh
cherries, pitted and chilled

SERVES 4–6

Put 500 ml (17 fl oz/2 cups) cold water and the sugar in a small saucepan. Sprinkle over the agar-agar. Bring the mixture to the boil and simmer for about 1 minute. Remove from the heat and add the evaporated milk and natural almond extract.

Pour the mixture into a shallow 18 x 28 cm (7 x 11¹/₂ inch) cake tin to set. Chill for at least 1 hour. Cut the jelly into diamond shapes, and serve with the fruit.

PREPARATION TIME: 5 MINUTES +   COOKING TIME: 5 MINUTES

NOTE: Agar-agar is similar to gelatine but does not need refrigeration to help it set. If it is unavailable, use 3 teaspoons of powdered gelatine sprinkled over 125 ml (4 fl oz/¹/₂ cup) cold water to soften. Stir the gelatine mixture into the water and sugar mixture, bring to the boil, then remove it from the heat — there is no need to simmer. Proceed with the method as above but refrigerate the jelly for 5 hours instead.

EIGHT-TREASURE RICE

12 whole blanched lotus seeds
(see Notes)

12 jujubes (dried Chinese dates)
(see Notes)

20 fresh or tinned gingko nuts, shelled
(see Notes)

225 g (8 oz) glutinous rice

2 tablespoons sugar

2 teaspoons oil

30 g (1 oz) slab sugar

8 glacé cherries

6 dried longans, pitted (see Notes)

4 almonds or walnuts

225 g (8 oz) red bean paste

SERVES 8

Soak the lotus seeds and jujubes in separate bowls of cold water for 30 minutes, then drain. Remove the seeds from the jujubes. If using fresh gingko nuts, blanch in a saucepan of boiling water for 5 minutes, then refresh in cold water and dry thoroughly.

Put the glutinous rice and 300 ml (10½ fl oz) water in a heavy-based saucepan and bring to the boil. Reduce the heat to low and simmer for 10–15 minutes. Stir in the sugar and oil. Dissolve the slab sugar in 210 ml (7½ fl oz) water and bring to the boil. Add the lotus seeds, jujubes and gingko nuts and simmer for 1 hour, or until the lotus seeds are soft. Drain, reserving the liquid.

Grease a 1 litre (35 fl oz/4 cup) heatproof bowl and decorate the base with the lotus seeds, jujubes, gingko nuts, cherries, longans and almonds. Smooth two-thirds of the rice over this to form a shell on the surface of the bowl. Fill with the bean paste, cover with the remaining rice and smooth the surface.

Cover the rice with a piece of greased foil and put the bowl in a steamer. Cover and steam over simmering water in a wok for 1–1½ hours, replenishing with boiling water during cooking. Turn the pudding out onto a plate and pour the reserved sugar liquid over the top. Serve hot.

PREPARATION TIME: 20 MINUTES +   COOKING TIME: 3 HOURS

NOTE: Lotus seeds are the seeds from the lotus and are available from Asian grocery stores.

Jujubes (Chinese dates) are an olive-sized dried fruit with a red, wrinkled skin. They are thought to be lucky because of their red colour.

Gingko nuts are the nuts of the maidenhair tree. The hard shells are cracked open and the inner nuts soaked to loosen their skins. Shelled nuts can be bought in tins and are easier to use than unshelled ones.

Longans are from the same family as lychees. They are available fresh, tinned or dried.

KULFI

1½ litres (52 fl oz/6 cups) milk
8 cardamom pods
4 tablespoons caster (superfine) sugar
20 g (¾ oz) blanched almonds, finely chopped
20 g (¾ oz) pistachio nuts, chopped, plus extra, to garnish
vegetable oil, for greasing

SERVES 6

Put the milk and cardamom pods in a large heavy-based saucepan, bring to the boil then reduce the heat and simmer, stirring often until it has reduced by about one-third, to 1 litre (35 fl oz/4 cups) — this will take some time. Keep stirring or it will stick.

Add the sugar and cook for 2–3 minutes. Strain out the cardamom pods and add the nuts. Pour the kulfi into a shallow metal or plastic container, cover the surface with a sheet of baking paper and freeze for 1 hour. Remove from the freezer and beat to break up any ice crystals, freeze again and repeat twice more.

Lightly brush six 250 ml (9 fl oz/1 cup) pudding basins (moulds) with the oil and divide the kulfi among them, then freeze overnight. To serve, unmould each kulfi and cut a cross ½ cm (¼ inch) deep in the top. Serve with extra pistachio nuts sprinkled over the top.

PREPARATION TIME: 20 MINUTES +   COOKING TIME: 50 MINUTES

DEEP-FRIED ICE CREAM IN COCONUT

2 litres (70 fl oz/8 cups) vanilla ice cream
1 egg
125 g (4½ oz/1 cup) plain (all-purpose) flour
150 g (5½ oz/1½ cups) fine dry breadcrumbs
2 tablespoons desiccated coconut
oil, for deep-frying

SERVES 6

Make six large scoops of ice cream and place them on a baking tray and return to the freezer.

Mix the egg, flour and 185 ml (6 fl oz/¾ cup) water in a bowl and stir thoroughly to make a thick batter. Coat the ice cream balls with the batter, then roll in the breadcrumbs and coconut to coat thickly. Return to the freezer and freeze for several days.

Fill a deep-fryer or large heavy-based saucepan one-third full of oil and heat to 180ºC (350ºF), or until a cube of bread dropped into the oil browns in 15 seconds. Slide in one ice-cream ball at a time and cook for a few seconds until the surface is golden. Take care not to melt the ice cream. Remove and serve immediately.

PREPARATION TIME: 20 MINUTES +   COOKING TIME: 10 MINUTES

SWEET WON TONS

125 g (4½ oz) dates, pitted and chopped
2 bananas, finely chopped
45 g (1¾ oz/½ cup) flaked almonds, lightly crushed
½ teaspoon ground cinnamon
60 won ton wrappers
oil, for deep-frying
icing (confectioners') sugar, to dust

MAKES 30

Mix together the dates, banana, almonds and cinnamon. Put 2 teaspoons of the fruit mixture into the centre of a won ton wrapper, and brush the edges lightly with water. Place another won ton wrapper on top at an angle so that the wrappers make a star shape. Place the won tons on a baking tray lined with baking paper. Repeat with the remaining ingredients, taking care not to stack the won tons on top of each other or they will stick together.

Fill a deep-fryer or large heavy-based saucepan one-third full of oil and heat to 180ºC (350ºF), or until a cube of bread dropped into the oil browns in 15 seconds. Deep-dry the won tons, in small batches for 2 minutes, or until crisp and golden. Drain on paper towel. Dust the won tons lightly with icing sugar before serving.

PREPARATION TIME: 15 MINUTES COOKING TIME: 20 MINUTES

CHINESE FORTUNE COOKIES

3 egg whites
60 g (2¼ oz/½ cup) icing (confectioners')
sugar, sifted
45 g (1½ oz) unsalted butter, melted
60 g (2¼ oz/½ cup) plain (all-purpose)
flour

MAKES ABOUT 30

Preheat the oven to 180ºC (350ºF/ Gas 4). Line a baking tray with baking paper. Draw three circles with 8 cm (3¼ inch) diameters on the paper.

Put the egg whites in a bowl and whisk until just frothy. Add the icing sugar and butter and stir until smooth. Add the flour and mix until smooth. Allow to stand for 15 minutes.

Using a flat-bladed knife, spread 1½ level teaspoons of the mixture over each circle. Bake for 5 minutes, or until slightly brown around the edges. Working quickly, remove the cookies from the tray by sliding a flat-bladed knife under each. Place a written fortune message on each cookie. Fold the cookie in half to form a semi-circle, then fold again over a blunt-edged object like the rim of a glass. Allow to cool on a wire rack. Repeat with the remaining mixture.

PREPARATION TIME: 40 MINUTES +   COOKING TIME: 50 MINUTES

NOTE: Cook no more than two or three cookies at a time, otherwise they will harden too quickly and break when folding.

COCONUT TAPIOCA

150 g (5½ oz/⅔ cup) pearl tapioca
875 ml (30 fl oz/3½ cups) coconut milk
1 vanilla bean
115 g (4 oz/½ cup) caster (superfine) sugar
coconut milk, extra, to serve
chopped pistachio nuts, to serve

SERVES 4

Put the pearl tapioca, coconut milk and vanilla bean in a large heavy-based saucepan. Stir over low heat for 15 minutes. Keep stirring so the tapioca doesn't stick and burn. Add the sugar and stir until dissolved. Remove the vanilla bean and transfer the tapioca to a bowl. Allow to cool, then refrigerate until cold.

Serve in small dishes with a little of the extra coconut milk poured over, and sprinkle with chopped pistachio nuts.

PREPARATION TIME: 10 MINUTES +   COOKING TIME: 15 MINUTES

SPICY COCONUT CUSTARD

2 cinnamon sticks
1 teaspoon freshly grated nutmeg
2 teaspoons whole cloves
310 ml (10¾ fl oz/1¼ cups) pouring
(whipping) cream
90 g (3¼ oz) chopped palm sugar
(jaggery), or soft brown sugar
270 ml (9½ fl oz) coconut milk
3 eggs, lightly beaten
2 egg yolks, lightly beaten
whipped cream, to serve
toasted flaked coconut, to serve

SERVES 8

Preheat the oven to 160ºC (315ºF/Gas 2–3). Combine the cinnamon, nutmeg, cloves, cream and 250 ml (9 fl oz/1 cup) water in a saucepan. Bring to simmering point, reduce the heat to very low and leave for 5 minutes to allow the spices to infuse the liquid. Add the sugar and coconut milk, return to low heat and stir until the sugar has dissolved.

Whisk the eggs and egg yolks in a bowl until combined. Stir in the spiced mixture, then strain, discarding the whole spices. Pour into eight 125 ml (4 fl oz/¼ cup) ramekins or dariole moulds. Place in a baking dish and pour in enough hot water to come halfway up the sides of the ramekins. Bake for 40–45 minutes until set. The custards should wobble slightly when the dish is shaken lightly. Remove the custards from the baking dish. Serve hot or chilled with whipped cream and toasted flaked coconut sprinkled over the top.

PREPARATION TIME: 20 MINUTES   COOKING TIME: 1 HOUR

GREEN TEA ICE CREAM

4 tablespoons Japanese green tea leaves
500 ml (17 fl oz/2 cups) milk
6 egg yolks
115 g (4 oz/1/2 cup) caster (superfine) sugar
500 ml (17 fl oz/2 cups) pouring (whipping) cream

SERVES 4

Combine the green tea leaves with the milk in a saucepan and slowly bring to simmering point. This step should not be rushed — the longer the milk takes to come to a simmer, the better the infusion of flavour. Set aside for 5 minutes before straining.

Whisk the egg yolks and sugar in a heatproof bowl until thick and pale, then add the infused milk. Place the bowl over a saucepan of simmering water, making sure that the base of the bowl does not touch the water. Stir the custard until it is thick enough to coat the back of spoon, then remove from the heat and allow to cool slightly before stirring through the cream. Transfer to an ice cream machine and freeze according to manufacturer's instructions. Alternatively, transfer to a shallow metal tray and freeze, whisking every couple of hours until frozen and creamy. Freeze overnight.

PREPARATION TIME: 15 MINUTES +   COOKING TIME: 30 MINUTES

NOTE: If you prefer your green tea ice cream pale green, add a few drops of green food colouring.

CHINESE ALMOND PUDDING

100 g (3½ oz/1 cup) ground almonds
90 g (3¼ oz/½ cup) glutinous rice flour
625 ml (21½ fl oz/2½ cups) milk
115 g (4 oz/½ cup) caster (superfine) sugar
fresh mango, to serve (optional)

SERVES 6

Combine the ground almonds and rice flour in a heavy-based saucepan and mix in about 80 ml (2½ fl oz/⅓ cup) cold water to form a thick, smooth paste. Add a little more water if necessary. Add the milk and stir until smooth.

Place the pan over low heat and cook, stirring almost constantly so that it does not catch, for about 1¼ hours, or until thick and smooth. Gradually add the sugar, stirring until dissolved. Pour the mixture into six small Chinese rice bowls. You can either serve the pudding warm, or allow to cool slightly, then refrigerate for 3 hours, or until firm. When chilled, it is delicious served with fresh mango.

PREPARATION TIME: 5 MINUTES +   COOKING TIME: 1 HOUR 15 MINUTES

INDEX

INDEX